Better Homes and Gardens®

# Knitting & Crocheting


First Edition. First Printing.
Library of Congress Catalog Card Number: 85-72758
ISBN: 0-696-01445-9

**BETTER HOMES AND GARDENS® BOOKS**

Editor: Gerald M. Knox
Art Director: Ernest Shelton
Managing Editor: David A. Kirchner
Copy and Production Editors: James D. Blume, Marsha Jahns, Rosanne Weber Mattson, Mary Helen Schiltz

Crafts Editor: Jean LemMon
Senior Crafts Books Editor: Joan Cravens
Associate Crafts Books Editors: Sara Jane Treinen, Judy Veeder

Associate Art Directors: Linda Ford Vermie, Neoma Alt West, Randall Yontz
Assistant Art Directors: Lynda Haupert, Harijs Priekulis, Tom Wegner
Senior Graphic Designers: Jack Murphy, Stan Sams, Darla Whipple-Frain
Graphic Designers: Mike Burns, Sally Cooper, Brian Wignall, Kim Zarley

Vice President, Editorial Director: Doris Eby
Executive Director, Editorial Services: Duane L. Gregg

Senior Vice President, General Manager: Fred Stines
Director of Publishing: Robert B. Nelson
Vice President, Retail Marketing: Jamie Martin
Vice President, Direct Marketing: Arthur Heydendael

**Knitting and Crocheting**
Crafts Editors: Joan Cravens, Sara Jane Treinen, Rebecca Jerdee
Contributing Editors: Coleen Bragg, Ciba Vaughan
Copy and Production Editor: Rosanne Weber Mattson, Carl Voss
Graphic Designer: Faith Berven
Electronic Text Processor: Donna Russell

If you've an adventurous spirit, by all means stick to your knitting—and to your crocheting. These lively, popular needlecrafts offer a wealth of excitement for both traditional and experimental stitchers.

Whether you're seeking designs for classic handcrafted sweaters, baby clothes or children's toys, bridal accessories, or gifts for the home, in KNITTING AND CROCHETING you'll find over 100 projects to make that will stir your imagination, develop your skills, and delight your family and friends.

We've included designs for vests, sweaters, caps, and accessories to stitch for men, women, and children. Here, too, are afghans, tablecloths, bedspreads, rugs, and pillows for your home. Or look for smaller, special projects, such as a delicate crocheted trinket box or a pair of whimsical knitted animals. Whatever your reason for stitching—for your own satisfaction or with a friend or family member in mind—each design is a warm personal expression sure to be treasured for a lifetime.

In addition to a rich variety of projects and patterns, you'll find three special sections to spark your own creativity by showing you new ways to look at crocheting and knitting design. And throughout the book, we've incorporated stitchery tips (including step-by-step how-to photographs explaining each of the basic knit and crochet stitches) to help you perfect your technique and to ensure successful completion of every project you choose to make.

# CONTENTS

*A Celebration of Color, Pattern, and Texture*

# DESIGNING WITH COLOR

***Mixing and matching colors is the easiest way to put your personal stamp on any project. Whether you select yarns and threads to match your decor, flatter your complexion, or please your child, every design becomes uniquely your own by the colors you choose to create it.***

These afghans offer excellent opportunities for experimenting with color. Soft shades reminiscent of sea and sand grace the crocheted design, *far left,* as well as the knitted throw, *near left.* You could just as easily stitch these afghans in your own palette of bright primaries or soft pastels.

Directions for both afghans and the projects shown on the following pages begin on page 14.

# DESIGNING WITH COLOR

Here's a quartet of perfect projects for the novice crocheter. Double-crochet shells in rainbow tints are worked in *rounds* for the granny square designs, *below,* and in *rows* for the striped pillow tops pictured *opposite.*

The granny square designs make wonderfully creative use of small amounts of leftover yarn. Almost any color in your scrap bag can be substituted for those shown, as long as the yarns are all of similar weights and textures. For the pillow on the right stitch 25 squares; for the one on the left, stitch 49.

Both of these designs call for squares in five colors plus white. The squares could be worked up or assembled in almost any combination to create new designs of your own choice—a field of random-color patches, for example, or a checkerboard pattern stitched in two colors.

To work the horizontal and vertical stripes of the outsize pillows at right, choose three favorite colors to mix with white, or substitute another color, such as black, to act as the unifying agent.

You may wish to select a pretty print fabric for the pillow bindings, and then choose yarns in coordinating colors for the stripes.

Naturally, the stripes can be executed in any width and length you choose, worked in random bands of color, or in carefully repeated patterns, as shown.

# DESIGNING WITH COLOR

Gone are the days when pastel shades and demure designs were *de rigueur* for the preschool set. The brilliant colors and fuss-free styling of the two pullovers pictured here are just the ticket for today's youngsters.

Perfect toppings for a walk in the park or a toddle around the duck pond, each of these whimsical sweaters sports its own little flock of feathered friends.

The just-ducky short-sleeve sweater, *left,* features a placket front with buttons and three plump ducks waddling across a magenta background. If magenta doesn't suit, change the background to complement your child's coloring—these sassy white ducks will look splendid against almost any bright shade.

"Great weather for ducks" describes the scene on the fun-loving sweater at right. The design features crayon-bright colors and four little ducklings paddling in a puddle beneath fluffy white clouds and a splattering of sunshowers.

Motifs on the sweater at *left* are worked in duplicate stitch after the front is complete. The scene on the sweater *opposite,* however, is knitted in as you stitch. (For more on duplicate stitch, see page 85.)

# DESIGNING WITH COLOR

Let this collection of cozy winter accessories tempt you to try your hand at a bit of color mixing on your own.

Follow the color combinations shown in the pictures, if you wish. But it's also fun to indulge your most colorful fancies, creating lively clashes, subtle contrasts, or unexpected pairings of color to warm up a cold winter landscape.

The luxurious spill of scarf shown here offers two full yards' worth of vibrant stripes in soft mohair yarn. Easy-to-work rows of half-double crochet make this design simple enough for any beginner to tackle successfully.

The pattern may be worked in a carefully orchestrated sequence of repeating colors, as shown. Or stitch it in random rows of color, using whatever mohair yarns you can find in your workbasket or on sale at your favorite needlecraft shop.

The striped mohair tam is crafted from the same yarns used in the scarf. Just knit this easy-to-stitch hat on circular needles for a quick-to-make, colorful gift for a friend or loved one.

The off-white knitted Irish cap features a twisted rib stitch that even an all-thumbs knitter can craft with ease.

Like the crocheted scarf at left, the knitted tams, mittens, and scarf pictured on this page all can be worked in any single color or combination of colors you fancy.

Stitched in rich red mohair yarn, the softly sculpted tam *below* is as plump and perfect as a ripe strawberry. Work it in your favorite shade, then top it off with a pom-pom in a matching or contrasting color.

The red-and-gray-striped tam, *below right,* and the multicolored tam, *right,* as well as the striped scarf accented with checkerboard edgings, and the Fair Isle mittens are other designs that adapt with ease to a variety of imaginative color schemes. And for some creative suggestions for other projects to knit using these patterns, particularly the mitten motifs, see pages 154–159.

## Knitted Sampler Afghan

Shown on pages 6–7.
Finished size is 64x48 inches.

**MATERIALS**
Bucilla Softex Knitting Worsted (4-ounce balls): 2 balls *each* of 4 complementary colors
Bucilla Horizon Knitting Worsted (2-ounce balls): 4 balls *each* of 4 complementary colors
Size 9 knitting needles, or size to obtain gauge given below
Cable needle
Size H aluminum crochet hook

**Abbreviations:** Page 217.
**Gauge:** 9 sts = 2 inches.

**INSTRUCTIONS**
The afghan shown is made of forty-eight 8-inch knitted squares. The squares are worked in the six patterns given below. Work each pattern in the eight shades of knitting worsted listed above. Block the finished squares before assembling them into the afghan.

To begin each square pattern, cast on 36 sts. Work Pattern 1 below until block measures 8 inches square. Bind off. Rep Pattern 1 with each of the 7 additional colors. Then work the 8-inch blocks in each of the eight colors using Pattern 2 below. Continue working all patterns with the eight colors until 48 blocks are completed.

PATTERN 1—*Row 1:* * K 1, p 1; rep from * across.
*Row 2:* Rep Row 1.
*Row 3:* * P 1, k 1; rep from * across.
*Row 4:* Rep Row 3. Rep these four rows for pat.

PATTERN 2—*Row 1:* * P 4, k 4; rep from * across, ending p 4.
*Row 2:* * K 4, p 4; rep from * across, ending k 4.
*Row 3:* * P 4, **sl next 2 sts to cable needle and hold in front of work, k next 2 sts, k 2 sts from cable needle—cable made.** Rep from * across, ending p 4.
*Rows 4 and 6:* Rep Row 2.
*Rows 5 and 7:* Rep Row 1.
*Row 8:* Rep Row 2. Rep these 8 rows for pat.

PATTERN 3—*Row 1:* * P 4, k 4; rep from * across, ending p 4.
*Row 2:* * K 4, p 4; rep from * across, ending k 4.
*Row 3:* Rep Row 1.
*Rows 4 and 5:* Rep Row 2.
*Row 6:* Rep Row 1.
*Row 7:* Rep Row 2.
*Row 8:* Rep Row 1. Rep these 8 rows for pat.

PATTERN 4—*Row 1:* Knit all sts across row.
*Row 2:* * K 1, insert right-hand needle through center st of previous row directly below next st on left-hand needle and knit it, removing both sts from left-hand needle. Rep from * across.
*Row 3:* Knit all sts.
*Row 4:* K 2, * k under the next st and sl both sts from left-hand needle, k 1. Rep from * across.
Rep these 4 rows for pat.

PATTERN 5—*Row 1:* K across.
*Row 2:* P across.
*Rows 3 and 4:* K across.
*Row 5:* P across.
*Row 6:* K across. Rep these 6 rows for pat.

PATTERN 6: K every row.

FINISHING: Sew, weave, or crochet squares together using photograph, pages 6–7 as a guide.

Join yarn in any corner, ch 1, work 3 sc in same place as join; * sc across edge to next corner; in corner st work 3 sc. Rep from * around; join to first sc. Work 3 more rounds of sc, working 3 sc in center sc of 3-sc corner grp; fasten off.

## Crocheted Bias Afghan

Shown on pages 6–7.
Finished size is 50x62 inches.

**MATERIALS**
Bucilla Softex Knitting Worsted (4-ounce balls): 8 ounces dark blue (A), 12 ounces light blue (C), 12 ounces cream (D), 8 ounces tan (F)
Bucilla Horizon Knitting Worsted (2-ounce balls): 8 ounces brown (B), 12 ounces blue (E)
Size H aluminum crochet hook

**Abbreviations:** Page 211.

**INSTRUCTIONS**
*Note:* Because of variations in yarn textures and working tensions, the inc and dec sequence given may not work for all crocheters. As you work the pattern, place the corner of the afghan atop a square table, or gauge the squareness against a large book or other object. If the work is wider than square, omit the inc every third row. If the work is narrower than square, add additional inc along the rows.

With A, ch 2; 3 sc in second ch from hook, ch 1, turn.

*Row 1:* Sc in each sc across to last sc, **2 sc in last sc—inc made;** ch 1, turn.

Rep row 1 until work measures 6 inches, measuring diagonally from the center of the longest side to the beg ch.

Change to B and rep Row 1 until total length measures 12 inches, measuring diagonally. Rep pat, changing colors every 6 inches until all six colors have been worked. End work at top of triangle.

At this point, change to A, make an inc in first st at top of triangle, work even across and down to last 2 sts of row, **draw up lp in each of**

**last 2 sts, yo, draw through 3 lps on hook—dec made;** ch 1, turn. *Next row:* Make a dec over first 2 sts, work even across to last st, make an inc in last st, ch 1; turn. Rep last 2 rows until stripe is 6 inches wide. Change to B, and rep the 2 rows until total length of the strips is 6 inches, ending at top side (right edge) of afghan.

Change to C. *Next row:* Dec 1 st over first 2 sts of row, work across to end, ch 1; turn. Rep this row until stripe is 6 inches wide. Change colors in sequence as established. Rep this row until 2 sts rem. Fasten off. Weave in all ends.

With E, sc 4 rnds around perimeter of afghan, making 3 sc in corners so that work lies flat. End off.

## Granny Square Pillow Tops

Shown on page 8.
Both pillows measure 18 inches square.

**MATERIALS** (to make 1 pillow)
Unger Roly-Sport yarn (1¾-ounce balls): 2 balls of white (W); 1 ball each of blue (B), green (G), purple (P), orange (O), yellow (Y), red (R)
Size F aluminum crochet hook
2¼ yards of 1½-inch-diameter cotton cording
½ yard contrasting 44-inch-wide fabric for covering cording
⅔ yards of 44-inch-wide ecru cotton fabric for pillow top and back
Polyester fiberfill

**Abbreviations:** Page 211.
**Gauge:** 1 square measures 2¼x2¼ inches.

**INSTRUCTIONS**

*Note:* Both pillow tops are worked the same. The difference between them is the number of squares in each top and the number of rounds in the borders. One top is made with 49 squares with 3 rounds for the border. The other has 25 squares with 8 rounds for the border. The border is added after all squares are assembled.

**For the top with 49 squares**

Make 16 white squares, 8 orange, 7 red, 6 *each* of green, purple, and yellow.

**For the top with 25 squares**

Make 16 white squares, 1 teal, and 2 *each* of green, purple, orange, and red.

GRANNY SQUARE: Ch 5, join with sl st to make ring.

*Rnd 1:* Ch 3, 2 dc in ring, (ch 1, 3 dc in ring) 3 times; ch 1, join with sl st to top of ch-3.

*Rnd 2:* Sl st in next 2 dc and into ch-1 sp; ch 3, in same sp work 2 dc, ch 1, 3 dc; (ch 1, in next ch-1 sp work 3 dc, ch 1, 3 dc) 3 times; ch 1, join with sl st to top of ch-3.

*Rnd 3:* Sl st in next 2 dc and into ch-1 sp; ch 3, in same sp work 2 dc, ch 1, 3 dc; (ch 1, in next ch-1 sp work 3 dc; ch 1, in next ch-1 corner sp work 3 dc, ch 1, 3 dc) 3 times; ch 1, in next ch-1 sp work 3 dc; ch 1, join to top of ch-3. Fasten off.

ASSEMBLY: Arrange squares in their appropriate order as shown on the diagram, *right,* and with matching yarn, working in the *back loops,* whipstitch the squares together.

BORDER (for the pillow top with 49 squares) *Rnd 1:* Join teal in any ch-1 corner sp, **ch 3, in same sp work 2 dc, ch 1, 3 dc—beg corner made;** * ch 1, in next ch-1 sp work 3 dc; rep from * across to next corner ch-1 sp; in corner ch-1 sp work 3 dc, ch 1, 3 dc. Work rem sides to correspond; join last ch-1 to top of ch-3 at beg of rnd.

*Rnds 2–3:* Sl st in next 2 dc and into ch-1 sp, work a beg corner and rep from * in Rnd 1 around. Fasten off at end of Rnd 3.

BORDER (for the pillow top with 25 squares). Work pat as for Rnds 1–2 above, working 2 rnds with white. Fasten off at end of Rnd 2 after joining last ch-1 to top of ch-3. Join yellow in any ch-1 corner sp, work a first corner, and work in pat as established for 2 rnds; fasten off. Join red in any ch-1 corner sp, work a first corner and work in pat as established for 4 rnds. Fasten off at end of fourth rnd.

ASSEMBLY: From the off-white fabric, cut 2 pieces, each measuring 19x19 inches to allow for ½-inch seams for the front and back of pillow. Cover cording with fabric and stitch to front of pillow top on ½-inch seam line. With right sides together sew front and back together, being careful the cording does not catch in the seam and leave an opening for turning. Trim seams; clip corners and turn. Stuff with fiberfill; sew opening closed. With matching sewing thread, whipstitch the crocheted piece atop the pillow front.

**GRANNY SQUARE PILLOWS**

| | | | | | | |
|---|---|---|---|---|---|---|
| O | Y | G | P | O | Y | R |
| R | P | | | | G | P |
| G | | O | | R | | O |
| Y | | | Y | | | G |
| O | | R | | O | | R |
| P | G | | | | P | Y |
| R | O | Y | P | R | G | O |

| | | | | |
|---|---|---|---|---|
| O | | | | R |
| | P | | G | |
| | | T | | |
| | G | | P | |
| R | | | | O |

## Striped Crocheted Pillows Tops

Shown on pages 8–9.
The finished size of the red, white, turquoise, and green pillow is 16½x17½ inches; finished size of the teal, white, turquoise, and lavender pillow is 15½x18½ inches.

**MATERIALS**
**For the red, white, turquoise, and olive green pillow**
Unger Roly-Sport yarn (1¾-ounce balls): 1 ball *each* of olive green, turquoise, red, and white
**For the lavender, white, turquoise, and teal pillow**
Unger Roly-Sport yarn (1¾-ounce balls): 1 ball *each* of lavender, white, turquoise, and teal
**For both pillows**
Size F aluminum crochet hook
(To make 1 pillow)
2¼ yards of 1½-inch diameter cotton cording
½ yard contrasting 44-inch-wide fabric for covering cording
⅔ yard of 44-inch-wide ecru cotton fabric for pillow top and back
Polyester fiberfill

**Abbreviations:** Page 211.
**Gauge:** 6 dc = 1 inch

**INSTRUCTIONS**
**For the red, white, turquoise, and olive green pillow**
With red, ch 52. *Row 1:* In fourth ch from hook work 2 dc; (ch 1, sk 2 ch, in next ch work 3 dc) 15 times, ch 1, sk 2 ch, dc in last ch; ch 3, turn.

*Row 2:* In first ch-1 sp work 2 dc; (ch 1, in next ch-1 sp work 3 dc) 15 times; ch 1, dc in top of turning ch. Fasten off, turn.

*Row 3:* Join white in top of last dc, ch 3, in first ch-1 sp work 2 dc; (ch 1, in next ch-1 sp work 3 dc) 15 times; ch 1, dc in top of turning ch; ch 3, turn.

*Row 4:* Rep Row 2; fasten off white; turn.

*Row 5:* With olive green, rep Row 3; fasten off; turn.

*Row 6:* Join turquoise in top of last dc, ch 3 and rep Row 2; fasten off. Turn.

*Row 7:* With olive green, rep Row 3; fasten off. Turn.

*Rows 8–9:* With white rep Row 3 then Row 2; fasten off.

Working in pat as established, rep color sequence two more times, beginning with red and ending with white, then work 2 more rows with red. Fasten off, turn.

BORDER *Rnd 1:* Join turquoise in sp between first 2 dc of last row, **ch 3, in same sp work 2 dc, ch 2, 3 dc—first corner made.** * Ch 1, 3 dc in next ch-1 sp; rep from * across to next corner lp (formed by ch-1 and dc), ch 1, in corner lp work 3 dc, ch 2, 3 dc. Working along the rem sides, work in pat as established, working the 3 dc around the turning ch (or last dc in row) and working 3 dc, ch 2, 3 dc for corners. Join last ch-1 with sl st to top of ch-3 at beg of rnd.

*Rnd 2–3:* Sl st in next 2 dc and into ch-2 sp. Work a first corner and continue around working ch-1 between each 3 dc-group and working 3 dc, ch 2, 3 dc in each ch-2 corner lp. Join last ch-1 to top of ch-3 at beg of rnd; at end of rnd 3, fasten off.

*Rnd 4–7:* Join olive green in any ch-2 corner sp, and work a first corner; work in pat as established. Fasten off.

ASSEMBLY: From the off-white fabric, cut 2 pieces, each measuring 17½x18½ inches to allow for ½-inch seams for the front and back of pillow. Cover cording with fabric and stitch to front of pillow top on ½-inch seam line. With right sides together sew front and back together, being careful the cording does not catch in the seam; leave an opening for turning. Trim seams, clip corners, and turn. Stuff with fiberfill; sew opening closed. With matching sewing thread, whipstitch the crocheted piece atop pillow front.

**For the lavender, white, turquoise, and teal pillow**
With teal, ch 52. Work Rows 1–3 as for above pillow, changing colors as follows: Work 3 rows teal, 2 rows white, 3 rows turquoise, 2 rows white, 3 rows lavender, 2 rows white, 2 rows teal, 2 rows turquoise, 3 rows lavender.

Reverse color sequence beginning with turquoise and work opposite end to correspond, ending with 3 rows teal.

BORDER: Work as for above pillow working 2 rnds with white, 1 rnd with lavender, 1 rnd turquoise, 1 rnd teal. Fasten off.

FINISHING: Cut pillow back and front from off-white fabric, each piece measuring 16½x19½ inches. Follow assembly instructions for above pillow to complete.

## Just-Ducky Knitted Sweater

Shown on page 10.
Directions are for Size 2; changes for Size 4 and Size 6 follow in parentheses. Chest = 22 (24, 26) inches.

**MATERIALS**
Pingouin Pingofine (50-gram skeins): 2 (3, 4) of No. 324 violet, or a suitable substitute
Small amounts of white, black, and yellow yarn in a matching weight
Sizes 1 and 2 knitting needles, or size to obtain gauge below
3 small buttons

**Abbreviations:** Page 217.
**Gauge:** With larger needles over st st, 31 sts = 4 inches; 40 rows = 4 inches.

**INSTRUCTIONS**

BACK: With smaller needles, cast on 84 (94, 102) sts. Work in k 1, p 1 ribbing for 2 inches. Change to larger needles and work in st st until total length measures 7 (8¾, 10¼) inches.

ARMHOLE SHAPING: Bind off 3 (4, 5) sts at beg of next 2 rows, then bind off 2 sts at beg of next 4 rows, then 1 st at beg of next 4 rows—66 (74, 80) sts. Continue in st st until total length measures 11 (13½, 15¼) inches, ending with wrong-side row.

NECK AND SHOULDER SHAPING: *Rows 1-2:* Keeping to pat, bind off 5 (6, 7) sts at beg of next 2 rows.

*Row 3:* Bind off 5 (6, 6) sts at beg of row; k across, binding off center 26 (30, 32) sts for back of neck.

*Row 4:* Bind off 5 (6, 6) sts at beg of row, p across left shoulder; attach a second skein of yarn to right shoulder, bind off 5 sts at neck edge and p across.

*Row 5:* Bind off 5 (5, 6) sts of right shoulder, bind off 5 sts at neck edge of left shoulder; k across.

*Row 6:* Bind off 5 (5, 6) sts of left shoulder.

FRONT: Work same as for back until length to armhole shaping equals that of Back.

PLACKET OPENING: Beg to shape armholes same as for Back. On first armhole dec row, bind off center 6 (8, 8) sts. On next row attach a second ball of yarn and begin to work upper front sections separately working both sides simultaneously. Finish armhole shaping as for back and continue in st st until total length of Front measures 9¾ (11¾, 13½) inches, ending with a wrong-side row.

NECK SHAPING: *Row 1:* K across left shoulder, binding off 8 sts at neck edge of right shoulder, k across right shoulder.

*Row 2:* P across right shoulder, binding off 8 sts at neck edge of left shoulder, p across left shoulder.

*Rows 3-4:* Work same as Rows 1-2, but bind off 3 sts at neck edges.

*Rows 5-6:* Bind off 2 sts at neck edges.

*Rows 7-8:* Bind off 1 (2, 2) st at neck edge. *For sizes 4 and 6 only:* Bind off 1 st at neck edge on 2 more rows for Size 4; 4 more rows for Size 6—15 (17, 19) sts each shoulder. Work even until length past beg of armholes equals that of Back.

SHOULDER SHAPING: Bind off 5 (6, 7) sts at beg of next 2 rows, then 5 (6, 6) sts at beg of next 2 rows, then bind off 5 (5, 6) sts.

SLEEVES: With smaller needles, cast on 50 (56, 62) sts. Work in k 1, p 1 ribbing for 1¼ inches. Change to larger needles and work in st st, inc 6 sts evenly spaced across row—56 (62, 68) sts. Continue in st st and inc 1 st at each end of every 2nd (4th, 4th) row 3 times—62 (68, 74) sts. Work even until sleeve measures 2¼ (3¼, 3¼) inches.

ARMHOLE SHAPING: Bind off 2 sts at each end of every right-side row 3 times. * Bind off 1 st at each end of next right-side row, then 2 sts at each end of next right-side row. Rep from * 4 (5, 6) times more, then bind off 3 sts at each end of next right-side row. Bind off rem 14 sts.

NECK BORDER: Sew shoulder seams. With right side facing and smaller needles, pick up and k 20 (24, 26) sts along right front neck, then 34 (38, 40) sts around back neck, and 20 (24, 26) sts along left front neck. work in k 1, p 1 ribbing for ¾ (1¼, 1¼) inch. Bind off loosely in ribbing.

LEFT FRONT PLACKET: With smaller needles, cast on 38 (40, 42) sts and work in k 1, p 1 ribbing for ¾ (1¼, 1¼) inch. Bind off loosely in ribbing.

RIGHT FRONT PLACKET: Beg same as for Left Front Placket. When length of work equals half of finished size of Left Front Placket, bind off 2 sts at 3 evenly spaced intervals for buttonholes.

*Next row:* Keeping to ribbing, cast on 2 sts above each group of bind-off sts of previous row. Complete same as for Left Front Placket. Sew bands to placket opening, lapping buttonhole placket over rem placket. Sew on buttons to correspond.

DUCK MOTIFS: Positioning duck motifs roughly in lower left corner of sweater front (see photograph), embroider ducks in duplicate stitch according to chart, *below.*

FINISHING: Sew body and sleeve side seams. Sew in sleeves.

**JUST-DUCKY SWEATER**

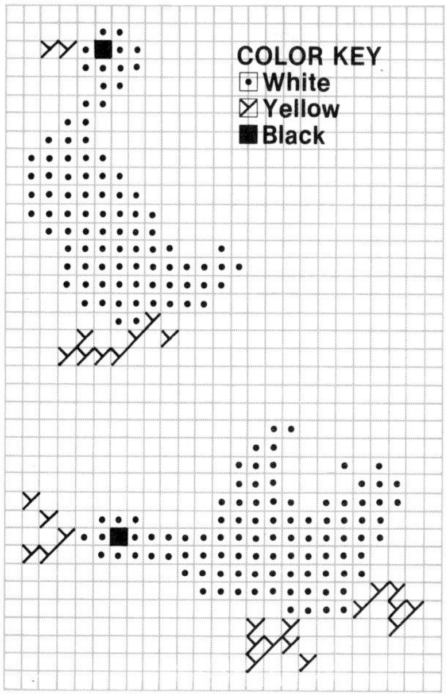


1 Square = 1 Stitch

# Great-Weather-for-Ducks Sweater

Shown on page 11.
Directions are for Size Small; changes for Size Medium and Size Large follow in parentheses. Chest = 24 (26, 28) inches.

**MATERIALS**
Pingouin Pingofine (50-gram skeins), or a suitable substitute, in the following amounts and colors: 3 (4, 4) of No. 370 magenta, 1 *each* of No. 330 yellow and No. 369 blue
1 (50-gram) skein of No. 27 white Pingouin Oued, or a suitable substitute
Sizes 2 and 5 knitting needles or size to obtain gauge given below
Size F aluminum crochet hook

**Abbreviations:** Pages 211 and 217.
**Gauge:** With larger needles over st st, 13 sts = 2 inches; 17 rows = 2 inches.

**INSTRUCTIONS**

FRONT: With smaller needles and magenta, cast on 70 (74, 78) sts. Work in k 1, p 1 ribbing for 1¾ inches. Change to larger needles and work 1 row more ribbing, inc 8 (10, 12) sts evenly spaced across—78 (84, 90) sts. Work 2 rows more st st.

Change to blue and beg pat by working 3 rows solid color. Continue in st st and follow chart, *opposite,* carrying color of yarn across back of work, being careful not to pull strands too tightly until 50 (52, 54) rows above ribbing have been completed.

ARMHOLE SHAPING: Bind off 2 sts at beg of next 2 rows—74 (80, 86) sts. Continue to work even in pat until 22 rows have been worked *past* beg of armhole.

**GREAT-WEATHER-FOR-DUCKS SWEATER**

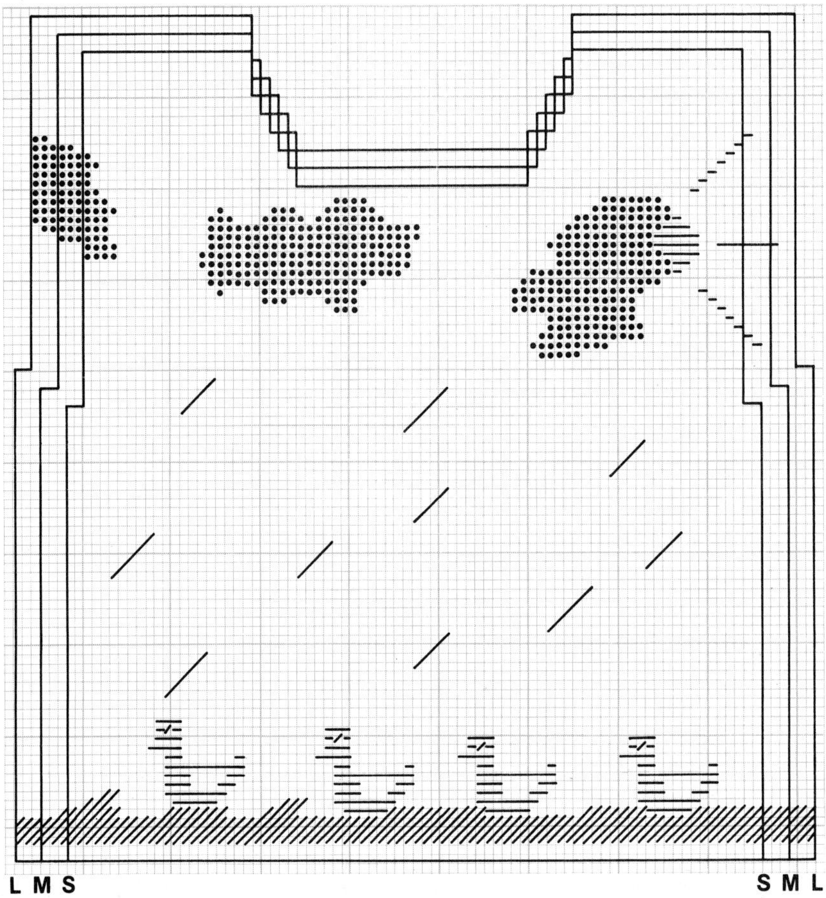


COLOR KEY
□ Magenta ⊡ White ⊟ Yellow ⊠ Blue

1 Square = 1 Stitch

NECK SHAPING: K 24 (27, 30) sts, bind off center 26 sts for neck, k 24 (27, 30) sts. On next row attach a second ball of yarn and work shoulder sections separately and simultaneously. Dec 1 st at each neck edge every other row 5 times—19 (22, 25) sts rem each shoulder. Work 4 rows even. Sl sts to holders (or bind off instead).

BACK: Work same as for Front, but in solid magenta, until length of armhole shaping equals that of Front. K 19 (22, 25) sts and sl to holder, bind off center 36 sts for back neck, k 19 (22, 25) sts and sl to holder (or bind off instead). Weave or sew shoulder sts tog.

RIGHT SLEEVE: With right side facing, larger needles, and blue, pick up 57 (63, 69) sts along right armhole edge. Work in st st for 4 inches or 1 inch less than desired sleeve length, ending with a p row. *Next row:* Dec 11 (15, 19) sts evenly spaced—46 (48, 50) sts. Change to smaller needle and work in k 1, p 1 ribbing for 1 inch. Bind off loosely in ribbing.

LEFT SLEEVE: Work as for Right Sleeve, substituting yellow yarn.

FINISHING: With right side facing and magenta, work 2 rnds sc around neckline of sweater. Sew sleeve and side seams.

# Knitted Bulky Irish Cap

Shown on page 12.

**MATERIALS**
Pingouin Iceberg (50-gram balls): 3 balls of ecru
Sizes 8 and 10 knitting needles

**Abbreviations:** Page 217.
**Gauge:** With larger needles, 7 sts = 2 inches.

**INSTRUCTIONS**
With smaller needles, cast on 76 sts.
*Row 1:* * P 1, k 2, p 1, k 1, rep from * across, end p 1.
*Row 2:* * K 1, p 1, k 1, p 2, rep from * across, end k 1.
*Row 3:* * P 1, k second st on left needle and leave on needle, k into skipped st and slide both sts off at one time, p 1, k 1 into row below, rep from * across, end p 1.
*Row 4:* Rep Row 2.
*Row 5:* * P 1, k 2, p 1, k 1 into row below, rep from * across, end p 1.
*Row 6:* Rep Row 2. Rep Rows 3–6 for pat until piece measures 6 inches from beg; end with a wrong side row, dec 4 sts evenly spaced across last row.
Change to larger needles and purl across. *Next row:* K across.
Continue in st st (k 1 row, p 1 row) until piece measures 2½ inches above ribbing. End with a purl row.
*Dec row:* * K 7, k 2 tog, rep from * across.
*Row 2:* Purl.
*Row 3:* * K 6, k 2 tog, rep from * across.
*Row 4:* Purl.
Continue dec on every right side row having 1 less st between decs until 8 sts remain. Cut yarn, leaving 15-inch tail. Run tail through rem sts, draw up tightly and secure. Use remaining tail to sew seam. Bury ends and add a 3-inch-diameter pom-pom to the top.

# Striped Mohair Tam

Shown on page 12.
Directions are for 21- to 24-inch head size.

**MATERIALS**
Kid Anny (50-gram skeins): 1 skein *each* of No. 254 red, No. 247 purple, and No. 1347 aqua
Anny Blatt Mohair and Silk (50-gram skeins): 1 skein of No. 1892 gold
Size 6 circular knitting needle (16 inches long), Size 9 circular knitting needle (24 inches long), and Size 9 double-pointed knitting needles, or size to obtain gauge given below.

**Abbreviations:** Page 217.
**Gauge:** With larger needles over st st, 7 sts = 2 inches.

**INSTRUCTIONS**
With smaller circular needle and purple, cast on 80 sts and join, being careful not to twist sts. Work in k 1, p 1 ribbing for 1½ inches. Change to larger circular needle. * K 1, inc in next st. Rep from * around—120 sts.
Work even in stripe pat using following colors for number of rnds indicated: 3 aqua, (1 purple, 1 aqua) twice, 3 gold, (1 aqua, 1 gold) twice, 3 purple, (1 red, 1 purple) twice, 3 aqua (1 gold, 1 aqua) twice, 3 red.
*Dec for top—first dec rnd:* With purple * k 8, k 2 tog. Rep from * around—108 sts. *Next rnd:* Work even 1 rnd with red. *Second dec rnd:* With purple * k 7, k 2 tog. Rep from * around—96 sts. *Next rnd:* Work even 1 rnd with red. Change to double-pointed needles when necessary.
Continue shaping as above, working 1 less st bet decs every other rnd and working in the following color pat in number of rnds indicated: 3 gold (1 red, 1 gold) twice, 3 purple, (1 aqua, 1 purple) twice—12 sts rem.
Next rnd: Continuing with purple, k 2 tog around, break off yarn and draw end through rem 6 sts. Pull tightly and fasten off. Steam hat to tam shape. *Do not stretch band.* When dry, brush well; add a 3-inch-diameter red pom-pom to top of tam.

# Crocheted Striped Muffler

Shown on page 12.
Finished size is 72 inches long.

**MATERIALS**
1 skein *each* of the following Anny Blatt Kid Anny mohair yarn (50-gram skeins), or a suitable substitute: No. 254 red, No. 247 purple, No. 1347 aqua, No. 534 yellow, and No. 272 black
Size I aluminum crochet hook, or size to obtain gauge below

**Abbreviations:** Page 211.
**Gauge:** 3 hdc = 1 inch.

**INSTRUCTIONS**
*Note:* Mohair yarn has a tendency to stretch after being worked. Beg ch may not look as long as necessary, but will stretch to size when scarf is completed.
With aqua, ch 242. *Row 1:* Hdc in third ch from hook and in each ch across; ch 2, turn.
*Row 2:* Sk first hdc, hdc in each hdc across and top of turning ch; drop aqua, draw yellow through lp on hook; ch 2; turn.
*Note:* Leave yarn ends free at ends of color-change rows and incorporate into fringe.
Continue as established, working 2 rows *each* of yellow, red, and purple; change to black and work as established for 2 rows, then work 2 rows of purple, red, yellow, and aqua. Fasten off.
Add 6-inch-long fringe.

## Knitted Four-Color Tam

Shown on page 13.
Directions are for 21- to 24-inch-circumference head size.

**MATERIALS**

Anny Blatt Sport Anny (100-gram skeins): 1 skein *each* No. 34 red, No. 1013 dark aqua, No. 1011 light aqua, and No. 56 gray
Size 6 circular knitting needle (16 inches long); Size 9 circular knitting needle (24 inches long)
Size 9 double-pointed needles
14-inch-diameter cardboard circle, aluminum foil

**Abbreviations:** Page 217.
**Gauge:** With larger needles over stockinette stitch, 4 sts = 1 inch.

**INSTRUCTIONS**

With red and smaller needle, cast on 80 sts; join, being careful not to twist sts. *Ribbing:* * K 1 through back lp, p 1. Rep from * around for 2 inches, making inc in each st on last rnd—160 sts.

Change to larger circular needle and st st (k 1 row, p 1 row) and * work 3 rnds in light aqua, gray, dark aqua, and red. Rep from * once; then work stripe in light aqua, gray, and dark aqua.

Keeping to stripe pat, dec for top as follows, changing to double-pointed needles when necessary: *Rnd 1:* * K 14, k 2 tog. Rep from * around. *Rnd 2:* * K 13, k 2 tog. Rep from * around. Continue to dec with 1 less st between dec every rnd until 20 sts rem.

*Next rnd:* K 2 tog around—10 sts. Break off all colors, leaving a 6-inch-long tail. Draw tail through rem sts, pull tightly and fasten off.

Block as for red and gray tam, page 21. Make a 3-inch-diameter pom-pom using all colors; sew to the top (see photograph, page 12).

## Knitted Fair Isle Mittens

Shown on page 13.
Directions are for child's large or woman's small. Measurement around mitten above thumb is 7½ inches.

**MATERIALS**

Brunswick Pomfret Sport Yarn (50-gram balls): 1 ball *each* of No. 591 blackberry heather (MC), No. 5142 light wisteria (A), No. 5031 medium yellow (B), No. 567 jade heather (C), and No. 557 cranberry (D)
Small amount of scrap yarn
Size 3 double-pointed needles

**Abbreviations:** Page 217.
**Gauge:** Over stockinette stitch, 7 sts = 1 inch.

**INSTRUCTIONS**

RIGHT MITTEN: With MC and double-pointed needles, cast on 40 sts on 3 needles; join, being careful not to twist sts. Work in k 1, p 1 ribbing for 2 inches, inc 12 sts evenly spaced on last rnd—52 sts. Change to st st (k 1 row, p 1 row), work Chart 1, *right,* for 3 inches, dec 2 sts on last rnd—50 sts. Break off MC and A.

THUMB OPENING: With B, k 2, k next 11 sts with scrap yarn; sl these 11 sts back to left needle and k them with B; complete rnd with B. Work even 1 rnd with B. Work Rows 1-13 of Chart 2, *right.*

With B, work even for two rnds, inc 2 sts on last rnd—52 sts. Break off B, C, and D. Resume Chart 1 with MC and A, working even for 1½ more inches.

**FAIR ISLE MITTENS**

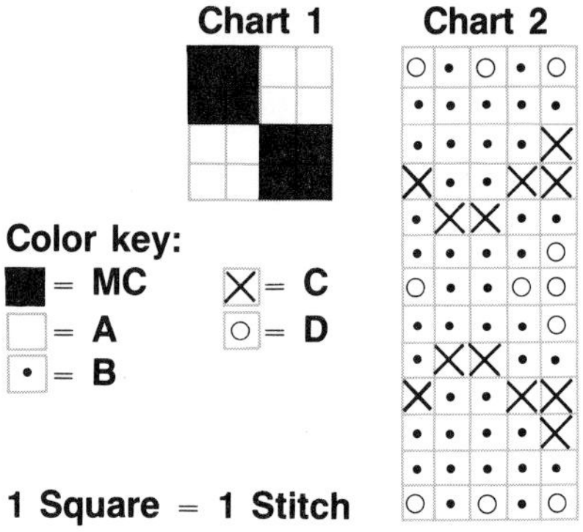


*Dec for top: Rnd 1:* * K 1, sl 1, k 1, psso, k 20, k 2 tog, k 1. Rep from * once.

*Rnd 2:* Work even, keeping to pat. Rep Rows 1-2, having 2 fewer sts bet decs on each dec rnd until 24 sts rem. Weave these sts tog. Fasten off.

THUMB: Remove scrap yarn. Slip 6 lps below opening (on right) to first needle, sl next 5 lps to second needle, sl 10 lps above opening to third needle—21 lps. Join MC and pick up 2 sts between third and first needle. Work across first and second needles, beg 2 sts with A, then following Chart 1. Keeping to pat, pick up 1 st between second and third needles and sl to third needle. Work across third needle—24 sts. Work even for 2 inches. K 2 tog around—12 sts. Work even 1 rnd.

Break off yarn, leaving 5 inches of MC. Run yarn through rem sts, pull tightly and fasten off.

LEFT MITTEN: Work as for right mitten to thumb opening.

*Thumb opening:* K with B to last 13 sts. K next 11 sts with scrap yarn. Sl these 11 sts back to left needle and k with B, k 2. Complete Left Mitten as for Right Mitten.

# Knitted Checked Muffler

Shown on page 13.
Finished size is 8¾x60 inches, excluding the fringe.

**MATERIALS**
Anny Blatt Sport Anny (50-gram skeins): 2 skeins *each* of No. 34 red and No. 56 pearl gray
Size 8 knitting needles
8 yarn bobbins
Backing fabric

**Abbreviations:** Page 217.
**Gauge:** Over stockinette stitch, 4 sts = 1 inch.

**INSTRUCTIONS**
Wind four yarn bobbins with red and four bobbins with gray. (*Note:* When changing colors, twist the new color around the color in use to prevent making holes in work.)

With red, cast on 35 sts. Work in st st (k 1 row, p 1 row) for 6 rows, ending with a wrong-side row.

CHECKERBOARD BAND: *Rows 1, 3,* and *5* (right side): * K 5 red, k 5 gray. Rep from * across, ending with k 5 red.

*Rows 2, 4,* and *6:* * P 5 red, p 5 gray. Rep from * across, ending with p 5 red.

*Rows 7, 9,* and *11:* * K 5 gray, k 5 red. Rep from * across, ending with k 5 gray.

*Rows 8, 10,* and *12:* * P 5 gray, p 5 red. Rep from * across, ending with p 5 gray.

Rep Rows 1-12 twice more; then rep Rows 1-6 once more.

STRIPE BAND: Keeping to st st as established, * work 6 rows red, 6 rows gray. Rep from * until total length measures approximately 51 inches (or about 9 inches less than the desired finished length), ending with a gray row.

CHECKERBOARD BAND: Work Rows 7-12 of Checkerboard Section—4 gray squares and 3 red squares. Then rep Rows 1-12 of Checkerboard Section 3 times.

Complete scarf with 6 rows of gray st st. Tie in all yarn ends; block. Line with fabric.

# Knitted Red Tam

Shown on page 13.
Directions are for 21- to 24-inch-circumference head size.

**MATERIALS**
Anny Blatt Kid Anny (50-gram skeins): 1 skein of No. 254 red
Anny Blatt Sport Anny (100-gram skein) 1 skein of No. 34 red
Sizes 6 and 10½ knitting needles

**Abbreviations:** Page 217.
**Gauge:** With larger needles and Kid Anny over pat st, 2 sts = 1 inch.

**INSTRUCTIONS**
With smaller needles and Sport Anny, cast on 79 sts.

*Row 1* (right side): * K 1 through back lp (tbl), p 1. Rep from * across, ending with k 1 tbl.

*Row 2:* * P 1, k 1 tbl. Rep from * across, ending with p 1. Rep Rows 1-2 for 1½ inches, ending with a wrong-side row and inc 6 sts evenly spaced on last row—85 sts.

Change to larger needles and Kid Anny Mohair. *Row 1:* * K 1 into row below, k 1. Rep from * across, end with k 1 into row below.

*Row 2:* * K 1, k 1 into row below. Rep from * across, ending with k 1. Rep Rows 1-2 until total length measures 8½ inches, ending with right-side row.

*Dec for top—Row 1* (wrong side): * P 1, p 2 tog. Rep from * across, ending with p 1—57 sts. *Row 2:* Knit. *Row 3:* P 2 tog across, end p 1—29 sts. *Row 4:* Knit. *Row 5:* P 2 tog across, ending with p 1—15 sts. *Row 6:* Knit.

*Row 7:* P 2 tog across, end p 1—8 sts rem.

Break off, leaving an 8-inch tail. Draw tail through rem sts and pull tightly. Fasten off. Sew seam. Make 3-inch-diameter red pom-pom and sew atop hat.

# Red and Gray Tam

Shown on page 13.
Directions are for 21- to 24-inch-circumference head size.

**MATERIALS**
Anny Blatt Sport Anny (100-gram skein): 1 skein *each* of No. 34 red and No. 56 gray
2 stitch markers; 14-inch-diameter cardboard circle, aluminum foil
Sizes 6 and 8 knitting needles

**Abbreviations:** Page 217.
**Gauge:** With Size 8 needles over stockinette stitch, 4 sts = 1 inch.

**INSTRUCTIONS**
With Size 6 needles and red, cast on 85 sts. *Row 1* (right side): * K 1 through back lp (tbl), p 1. Rep from * across, end k 1 tbl. *Row 2:* * P 1, k 1 tbl. Rep from * across, end p 1. Rep Rows 1-2 for 1½ inches, end with p row.

Alternating 2 rows of gray and 2 rows of red, change to Size 8 needles and st st, inc 3 sts evenly spaced on next row—88 sts. Work in st st for 1 inch, end with p row.

*First inc row:* K 7, inc in next st, place marker, * k 10, inc in next st, place marker. Rep from * across, end k 3—96 sts. Work even for 1 inch, end with p row.

*Second inc row:* * K to 1 st before marker, inc in next st, sl marker. Rep from * across, end k 3—104 sts. Work even for 1 inch, end with p row. Rep second inc row twice more, working even 1 inch after each inc row. Work 1 more inc row, work even for 2 inches—128 sts.

*First dec row:* * K to 2 sts before marker, k 2 tog. Rep from * across. *Row 2:* Purl. Rep Rows 1-2 until 8 sts rem. Break off yarn, leaving 14-inch tails. Draw one tail through rem sts, pull tightly and fasten off. Use rem tail to sew seam.

*Blocking:* Cover cardboard with foil, slip into hat and steam hat to tam shape; let dry. Remove cardboard. Make pom-pom with red and gray; sew to top.

*A Celebration of Color, Pattern, and Texture*

# PLAYING WITH PATTERN

***Increasing and decreasing stitches from row to row, changing stitch patterns, and altering yarn colors on cue are all ways of using pattern to shape design. This section explores a few of these possibilities.***

Careful patterning shapes the knitted pillow dolls, *left,* and their plump pet pony, *above.* Though the designs appear to be intricate, you can work these toys entirely in stockinette stitch and shape the bodies with simple increases and decreases. To stitch the dolls' costumes and create clothing and accessories just change yarn colors. Finish each doll with a flourish of embroidery and felt appliqués. Directions begin on page 28.

# PLAYING WITH PATTERN

Named for a branch of the Campbell clan of Scotland, whose tartan inspired the original design, argyle patterns have long been a favorite with knitters. Traditionally, argyle designs appear on knitted socks and sweaters. Here are two adventurous adaptations of this popular motif.

The knitted rug, *below,* features a stylized arrangement of argyle stripes and diamonds. A similar design is embroidered onto afghan-stitch panels set into the lavishly textured crocheted throw, *opposite.*

You can work the rug below in stockinette stitch, but knit the inside periwinkle borders in seed stitch. Complete this 33x37-inch rug using duplicate stitch for the diagonal stripes.

For the 57x66-inch throw at *right,* crochet two afghan-stitch panels and embellish them with cross-stitched argyle motifs. Assemble them between three panels of popcorns arranged in diamonds and flanked by classic cables.

# PLAYING WITH PATTERN

Scottish tartans also inspired these stylish sweaters, but the designs are far from traditional. The patterns appear to be complex, but the technique used to stitch them is amazingly easy, and the results are stunning.

To create each plaid design, knit the horizontal stripes of the pattern in stockinette stitch while working the front of each sweater. Add the vertical stripes in duplicate stitch after completing the pieces of the sweater.

Once you've mastered this simple "plaiding" technique, have a fling at changing the color combinations and stripe arrangements to create new tartan designs of your own. On page 35 you'll find some tips to get you started.

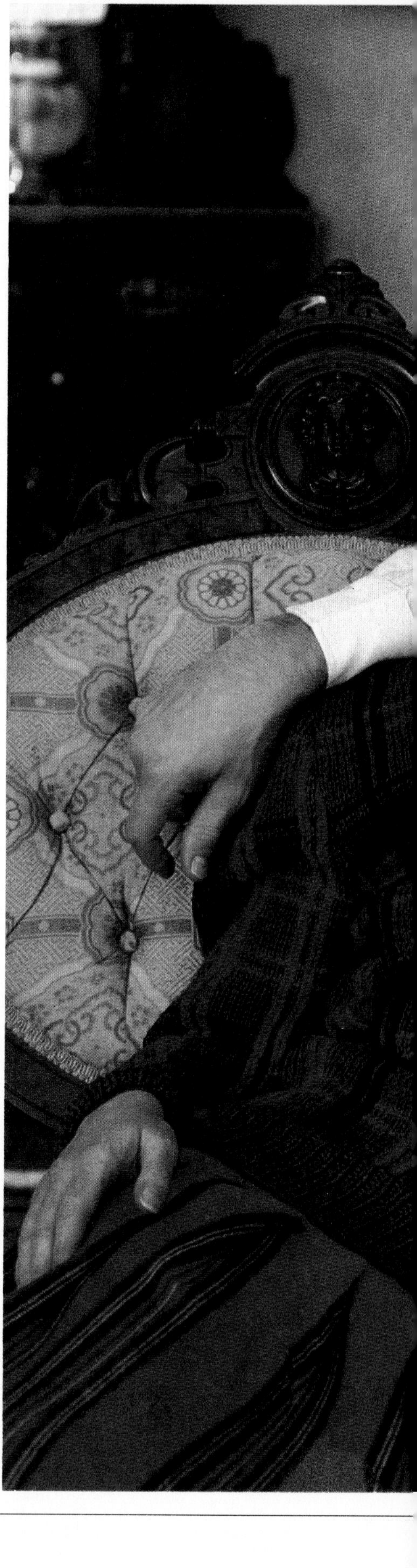

# Knitted Pillow Dolls and Horse

Shown on pages 22–23.
Finished size of dolls is approximately 17 inches tall. Horse is about 14 inches long.

**MATERIALS**
Brunswick Germantown Knitting Worsted yarn (100-gram skeins): 1 skein *each* of No. 400 snow white, No. 424 cardinal, No. 444 Dartmouth green, No. 460 black, No. 4051 saffron, and No. 4182 light oriental rose
Felt scraps, sewing thread
Embroidery floss, tapestry needle
Fiberfill
Size F crochet hook
Size 8 knitting needles

**Abbreviations:** Page 217.
**Gauge:** Over stockinette stitch (st st), 4 sts = 1 inch; 6 rows = 1 inch.

**INSTRUCTIONS**
**For the girl doll**
FRONT: With black, cast on 34 sts. Work even in st st (knit one row; purl one row) through Row 6.
*Rows 7, 9, 11,* and *13:* Dec 1 st each side—26 sts.
*Row 14:* Change to white yarn, p.
*Rows 15–20:* Work even in st st.
*Rows 21, 23,* and *25:* P (right side).
*Rows 22, 24,* and *26:* K (wrong side).
*Row 27:* Change to rose yarn, k.
*Rows 28–30:* Work even in st st.
*Rows 31* and *32:* Cast on 4 sts at end of each row.
*Rows 33* and *34:* Inc 1 st each side—38 sts.
*Rows 35–40:* Work even.
*Row 41:* Change to white yarn, k.
*Rows 42–64:* Work even.
*Rows 65, 67, 69,* and *71:* Dec 1 st each side. Work even on even-numbered rows.
*Rows 72* and *73:* Bind off 6 sts at beg of each row—18 sts.
*Row 74:* Change to rose yarn, p.
*Rows 75, 77, 79,* and *81:* Inc 1 st each side—26 sts. Work even on even-numbered rows.
*Rows 82–90:* Work even.
*Row 91:* Change to saffron yarn, knit.
*Rows 92–94:* Work even.
*Rows 95, 97, 99,* and *101:* Dec 1 st each side.
Bind off 18 sts.

BACK: Work as for Front, except change to saffron on Row 74 and work back of head through Row 101 with saffron.

FRONT SKIRT AND APRON BODICE: With green, cast on 24 sts. Work even in st st through Row 22. *Row 23:* Change to cardinal, p.
*Row 24:* K. *Row 25:* P. *Row 26:* K.
*Rows 27–34:* Continue with cardinal, but work in st st.
*Row 35:* K 3, place rem 21 sts on holder. Work in st st on 3 sts through Row 41; bind off. Attach cardinal, bind off center 18 sts on holder and work rem 3 sts for strap to correspond.

BACK SKIRT AND APRON BODICE: Work as for Front through Row 26. *Row 27:* K 3. Place rem 21 sts on holder. Work in st st on 3 sts through Row 41. Bind off.

Attach cardinal, bind off center 18 sts and complete other strap.

APRON SKIRT: With cardinal, cast on 18 sts. *Rows 1, 2, 3,* and *5:* Knit. *Rows 4* and *6:* K 2, p 14, k 2.
*Rows 7, 8,* and *9:* Knit. *Rows 10–22:* Work even in st st, always k the first and last 2 sts. Bind off.

**For the boy doll**
FRONT: Follow directions for girl, except work Rows 21-26 and Rows 41-46 in st st following color chart, page 29.

SHORTS (Make 2): With green, cast on 24 sts. Work even in st st through Row 20. *Row 21:* K 3, place rem 21 sts on holder.
*Rows 22–46:* Working on 3 sts, k every row. Bind off. Attach green yarn, bind off center 18 sts, and complete other strap to correspond.

CROSS-PIECE FOR SHORTS (Make 1): With green, cast on 19 sts. Work 6 rows in st st following color chart, *right,* adding one extra stitch to chart so pattern will be even. Bind off 19 sts.

**To finish the boy and girl**
GIRL: Sew apron to skirt and apron bodice. Using yarn, appliqué skirt, apron bodice and straps to

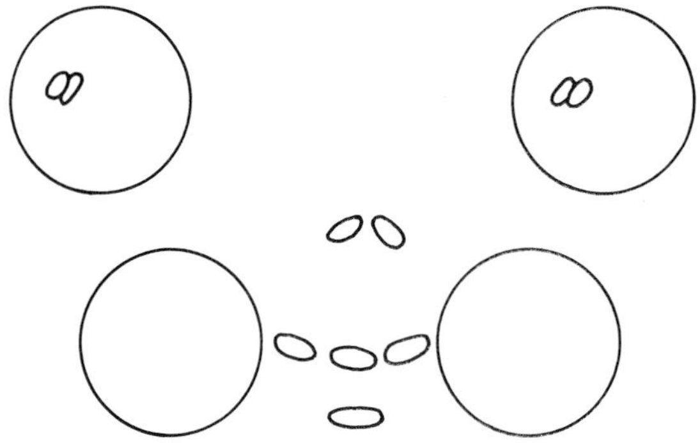

DOLL FACE — Full-size

front and back of doll pieces.

Using knitting worsted split into two strands, embroider around sleeves and neck with cross-stitches and backstitches, see chart, *right,* and apron with saffron cross-stitches and green backstitches. Begin backstitches on the *sleeves* one row in from rose row; and on the *neck,* two rows from rose row. With green yarn, crochet a chain 31 inches long for necktie.

Sew doll front to back; stuff with fiberfill. With thread, sew running stitches through front and back of doll to delineate legs and arms.

Beginning at neck center, weave crocheted chain through neck over and under two sts and tie in bow.

For hair, cut 24 strands of saffron yarn, each 60 inches long. Fold strands in half, tie at center. Separate into three groups of 16 strands each and braid. Sew braid around back of head, cutting off excess and tucking in ends.

Following diagram, *left,* cut eyes and cheeks from felt. Stitch in place and embroider mouth and nose with 6 strands of embroidery floss.

BOY: Sew crosspiece to shorts straps. Complete as for the girl doll, except omit embroidery at neck and sleeves. Crochet a cardinal chain for necktie.

**To make the horse**

*Note:* "Right edge" and "left edge" refer to edges of work as they face you.

With black, cast on 14 sts. Work even in st st through Row 4.

*Row 5:* Change to cardinal, k. Work in st st through Row 18.

*Rows 19* and *21:* Inc 1 st at left edge. At end of Row 21, place rem 16 sts on holder.

Make another leg, but inc at right edge on Rows 19 and 21.

*Row 22:* P 16 leg sts. Cast on 9 sts. P 16 sts from holder—41 sts.

Work even in st st through Row 36. *Rows 37, 39, 41,* and *43:* K 1, inc 1 st at right edge and dec 1 st at left edge. P even-numbered rows.

*Row 44:* Cast on 10 sts at end of row. P next row.

*Row 45:* K across, dec 1 st at left edge. P next row.

*Row 47:* K, inc 1 st at right edge and dec 1 st at left edge.

*Row 48:* Bind off 21 sts. P rem 29 sts. *Row 49:* Inc 1 st at right edge and dec 1 st at left edge. P next row.

*Rows 51 through 69:* Work in st st, dec 1 st each edge every row 7 times. Dec 1 st each end every other row 6 times. Bind off rem 3 sts.

Make another side, reversing shapings.

BLANKET: Cast on 14 sts with green. *Rows 1–4:* K. *Row 5:* K 2, inc in next st, k 8, inc in next st, k 2.

*Row 6:* K 2, p 12, k 2.

*Row 7:* K 2, inc 1 st in next st, k 10, inc 1 st in next st, k 2.

*Rows 8 through 34:* Work even in st st but always k first and last 2 sts of each row.

*Row 35:* K 2, dec 1, k 10, dec 1, k 2. *Row 36:* K 2, p 12, k 2.

*Row 37:* K 2, dec 1, k 8, dec 1, k 2.

*Row 38:* K 2, p 10, k 2. *Rows 39 through 42:* K. Bind off rem 14 sts.

FINISHING: Using chart, *below,* embroider blanket using lazy daisy and backstitches. (See photograph, page 22.) Sew horse together, leave opening for stuffing; stuff with fiberfill. Sew opening closed. Sew blanket on horse.

Make four saffron tassels by wrapping yarn 10 times around a 4-inch piece of cardboard. Remove from cardboard. Wrap another strand 6 times around the tassel ½ inch from center. Trim; sew tassels to corners of blanket.

With black, make mane by sewing backstitches through neck seam, leaving 2-inch-long ends on each side of each stitch.

Sew on eyes. With black, crochet a chain 18 inches long for rein. Embroider the bit; sew reins to the horse (see photograph). For tail, wrap black yarn 36 times around a 5½-inch piece of cardboard. Tie through center. Sew to the horse.

**KNITTED BOY'S TRIM**

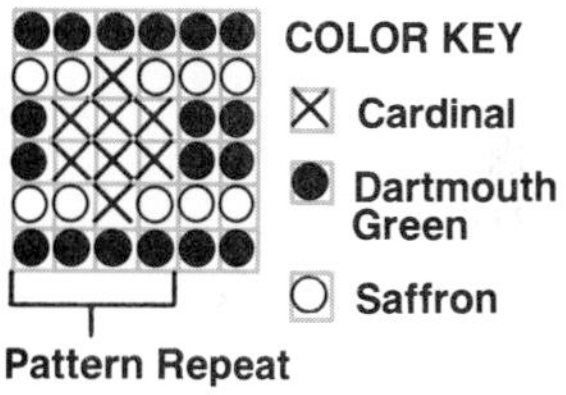


**CROSS-STITCHED GIRL'S TRIM**

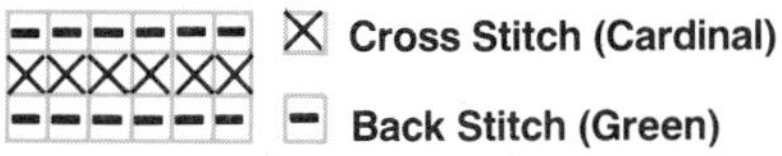


1 Square = 1 Stitch

SADDLE BLANKET

Full-size

## Knitted Argyle Rug

Shown on page 24.
Finished size is 33x37 inches.

**MATERIALS**

Paternayan Persian Yarn (178-yard hanks): 6 hanks of No. 511 blue, 4 hanks of No. 321 wine, 8 hanks of No. 203 gray, 3 hanks of No. 340 periwinkle
Size 10 circular knitting needle
Yarn bobbins
Size J aluminum crochet hook

**Abbreviations:** Page 217.
**Gauge:** 7 sts = 2 inches, 5 rows = 1 inch.

**INSTRUCTIONS**

*Note:* Using double strands of yarn throughout, work the rug in stockinette stitch (k 1 row, p 1 row), except for the periwinkle borders. Work these borders in seed stitch (* k 1, p 1, rep from * across row). Add periwinkle crossbars after the knitting is completed, working duplicate stitching over 2 rows of knitting.

With periwinkle, cast on 116 sts. Work 9 rows in seed stitch. At end of last row, end off periwinkle.

Before working from chart, *below,* wind 12 bobbins, 4 with gray yarn, 5 with blue, 3 with wine. Begin to work from chart and establish argyle pattern as follows: K 14 sts with blue, * join gray bobbin, k 1 st; join blue, knit 28 sts; rep from * 2 times more; join gray bobbin, k 1 st; join blue, knit 14 sts.

Continue to work from chart, being careful to twist the new color around the color in use to prevent holes in work where color changes occur. Work through Row 29 ending on a right side row.

*Row 30:* Work across 29 sts in pat from chart, join periwinkle and *knit* 58 sts to begin inside border, complete row in argyle pat.

*Row 31:* Work across 29 sts in pat from chart; with periwinkle, work over next 58 sts in seed stitch. Complete row in argyle pat.

Continue from chart working the

COLOR KEY: ▣ Blue ☐ Grey ▨ Wine ◘ Seed sts in Periwinkle ■ Duplicate sts in Periwinkle

1 Square = 1 Stitch

inside borders in seed stitch. When chart is completed, turn it upside down and rep rows in reverse order to work remaining half of rug.

*Note:* When you begin the 8 rows of the inside periwinkle border, knit the first row and begin the seed st on the second row.

When chart is completed, knit across all sts with periwinkle, then work 8 rows of border in seed stitch. Bind off.

Following chart, work duplicate stitches over 2 rows of knitting to complete argyle pat. See page 85 for duplicate stitch how-to.

Weave in all ends on wrong side. Steam block and allow rug to dry. With right side facing, join gray and work sc evenly spaced along long side edge only, ch 1, work 1 row *reverse sc* (work clockwise) in each sc across row. Fasten off. Repeat 2 rows of sc on opposite side of rug.

# Irish Crochet Argyle Afghan

Shown on pages 24–25.
Finished size is 57x66 inches.

**MATERIALS**

Unger Roly Poly worsted weight yarn (3½-ounce skeins): 17 skeins of off-white, plus 2 additional skeins for the fringe
Size H aluminum crochet hook
Size H aluminum afghan hook
Tapestry needle
Unger Roly Sport (50-gram skeins): 1 skein *each* of maroon, rose, and gray

**Abbreviations:** Page 211.

**INSTRUCTIONS**

*Note:* Afghan is worked in five panels, then panels are sewn together. On the three Irish crochet panels, when working the trc around the post on the *right side* of the work, work the trc from the *front.* When working trc around the post on the *wrong side,* work the trc from the *back.*

**For the Irish crochet panels (make 3)**

With Size H crochet hook, ch 43.

*Row 1* (wrong side): Dc in the fourth ch from the hook and in each ch across; ch 3, turn.

*Row 2* (right side): *Note:* Popcorn sts are worked in groups of 4 dc. **Work 4 dc in the appropriate st, drop the lp from the hook, insert the hook from the *front* into the first dc of the 4-dc group and draw the dropped lp through, ch 1—pc made.**

Sk first dc, pc in next dc, dc in next 2 dc, **(sk next 2 dc, trc around post of next dc, trc around post of the second skipped dc; trc around the post of first skipped dc, sk 3 dc behind trc post sts) twice—2 cables made.** Dc in each of next 2 dc; pc in next dc; (dc in next 7 dc, pc in next dc) twice; dc in next 2 dc; work 2 cables over next 6 dc, dc in next 2 dc; pc in next dc, dc in turning ch-3 lp; ch 3, turn.

*Row 3: Note:* When working a popcorn on the *odd-numbered rows,* work as above, *except,* insert the hook from the *back* into the first dc of the 4-dc group and draw the dropped lp through, ch 1.

Work pc over pc, dc in 2 dc; trc around post of next 6 trc *from the back;* dc in 2 dc, pc over pc; dc in 6 dc, pc in next dc, dc in top of pc; pc in next dc; dc in 6 dc, pc over pc, dc in 2 dc; trc around post of next 6 trc *from the back;* dc in 2 dc, pc over pc, dc in turning ch-3 lp; ch 3, turn.

*Row 4:* Pc over pc; dc in 2 dc; 2 cables over next 6 trc, dc in 2 dc; pc over pc; dc in 5 dc; (pc in next dc; dc in top of pc) twice; pc in next dc; dc in 5 dc; pc over pc; dc in 2 dc; 2 cables over 6 trc; dc in 2 dc, pc over pc, dc in turning ch-3 lp; ch 3, turn.

*Row 5:* Pc over pc, dc in 2 dc; trc around post of next 6 trc from back; dc in 2 dc; pc over pc; dc in 4 dc, (pc in next dc, dc in top of pc) 3 times; pc in next dc; dc in 4 dc; pc over pc; dc in 2 dc; trc around post of next 6 trc from back; dc in 2 dc; pc over pc, dc in turning ch-3 lp; ch 3, turn.

*Row 6:* Pc over pc; dc in 2 dc; 2 cables over next 6 trc; dc in 2 dc; pc over pc; dc in 3 dc; (pc in next dc, dc in top of pc) 4 times; pc in next dc; dc in 3 dc; pc over pc; dc in 2 dc; 2 cables over next 6 trc; dc in 2 dc; pc over pc, dc in turning ch-3 lp; ch 3, turn.

*Row 7:* Pc over pc; dc in 2 dc; trc around post of next 6 trc from the back; dc in 2 dc; pc over pc; dc in next 3 dc and top of pc; (pc in next dc, dc in top of pc) 4 times; dc in next 3 dc; pc over pc; dc in 2 dc, trc around post of next 6 trc from back, dc in 2 dc; pc over pc, dc in turning ch-3 lp; ch 3, turn.

*Row 8:* Pc over pc; dc in 2 dc; 2 cables over next 6 trc; dc in 2 dc; pc over pc; dc in 4 dc and top of pc; (pc in next dc, dc in top of pc) 3 times; dc in 4 dc; pc over pc; dc in 2 dc; 2 cables over 6 trc, dc in 2 dc, pc over pc, dc in turning ch-3 lp; ch 3, turn.

*Row 9:* Pc over pc; dc in 2 dc; trc around post of next 6 trc from the back; dc in 2 dc; pc over pc; dc in 5 dc and top of pc; (pc in next dc, dc in top of pc) twice; dc in next 5 dc; pc over pc; dc in 2 dc, trc around post of next 6 trc from the back, dc in 2 dc; pc over pc, dc in turning ch-3 lp; ch 3, turn.

*Row 10:* Pc over pc; dc in 2 dc; 2 cables over next 6 trc; dc in 2 dc; pc over pc; dc in 6 dc and top of pc; pc in next dc, dc in top of pc and next 6 dc; pc over pc; dc in 2 dc; 2 cables over next 6 trc; dc in 2 dc; pc over pc; dc in turning ch-3 lp; ch 3, turn.

*Row 11:* Pc over pc; dc in 2 dc; trc around post of next 6 trc from the back; dc in 2 dc; pc over pc; dc in 7 dc, dc in top of pc, dc in 7 dc, pc over pc; dc in 2 dc, trc around post of next 6 trc from back, dc in 2 dc; pc over pc, dc in turning ch-3 lp; ch 3, turn.

*Row 12:* Pc over pc, dc in next 2 dc, work 2 cables over next 6 trc; dc in next 2 dc; pc over pc; (dc in next 7 dc, pc in next dc) twice; dc in next 2 dc; work 2 cables over next 6 trc, dc in next 2 dc; pc in next dc, dc in turning ch-3 lp; ch 3, turn.

Rep Rows 3–12 eleven more times, until 12 pc designs are complete. Fasten off.

*continued*

**For the embroidered afghan stitch panel (make 2)**

With Size H afghan hook, ch 35.

*First half of Row 1:* Leaving all lps on hook, sk first ch, * insert hook in next ch, yo, draw up lp; rep from * in each ch across—35 lps on hook.

*Second half of Row 1:* Yo, draw through first lp on hook, * yo, draw through next 2 lps on hook; rep from * across row until 1 lp rem on hook.

*First half of Row 2:* Insert hook around *second* vertical bar of Row 1, yo, draw up lp and leave on hook; * insert hook around next vertical bar, yo, draw up lp and leave on hook; rep from * across row to within 1 bar from end; insert hook around last bar and thread behind it, yo, draw up lp—35 lps on hook.

*Second half of Row 2:* Rep second half of Row 1. Rep Row 2 (first and second halves) until 206 rows are complete.

*Last row:* Draw up lp under second vertical bar and draw through lp on hook—1 lp rem on hook; * draw up lp in next vertical bar and draw through lp on hook—1 lp rem on hook; rep from * to within 1 bar from end; insert hook around last vertical bar and thread behind it, draw up lp and draw through lp on hook; fasten off.

CROCHETED ARGYLE AFGHAN

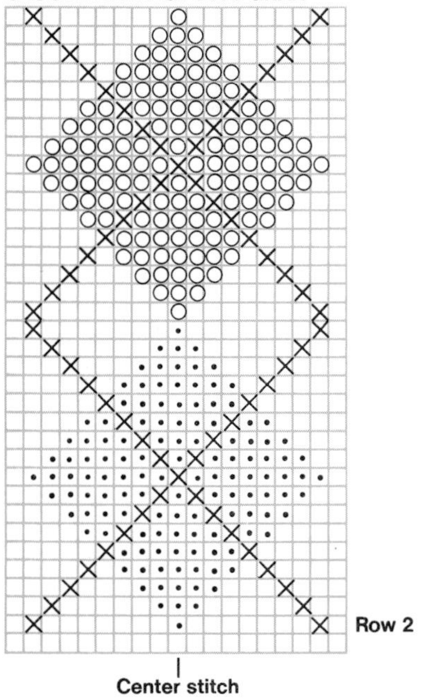


1 Square = 1 Stitch

COLOR KEY:

☒ Maroon

⊡ Rose

◯ Gray

CROSS-STITCH EMBROIDERY: To add the argyle pattern, follow chart, *left.* Using one strand of sport-weight yarn threaded into the tapestry needle, begin cross-stitching in the center stitch of the panel and on the *second* row of afghan sts. When making the cross-stitches, work sts over the upright bars; each cross-stitch should cover one upright bar. Repeat the charted design six times, working from bottom of panel to top.

**To finish the afghan**

Whipstitch embroidered panels between Irish crochet panels. Block the assembled afghan.

For the fringe, cut 14-inch lengths of yarn. Working with bundles of 8 strands each, knot strands into afghan at 1-inch intervals along top and bottom edges. Trim ends of fringe.

## Woman's Plaid Cardigan

Shown on pages 26–27.
Instructions are for Size Small (8-10); changes for Size Medium (12-14) and Size Large (16) follow in parentheses. Finished bust = 34½ (37, 41) inches.

**MATERIALS**

Coats & Clark Royal Mouliné worsted wool (50-gram balls), or a suitable substitute, in the following amounts and colors: 9 (10, 11) balls of No. 6009 royal blue, 2 balls *each* of No. 6001 red and No. 6006 spruce green

Sizes 6 and 9 knitting needles, or size to obtain gauge given below

3 stitch holders

Tapestry needle

7 buttons

**Abbreviations:** Page 217.

**Gauge:** With larger needles over st st, 9 sts = 2 inches; 13 rows = 2 inches.

**INSTRUCTIONS**

*Note:* The horizontal stripes are worked in st st as you knit the sweater. Join and break off red and spruce as needed. The vertical stripes are worked in duplicate sts when Back, Front, and Sleeves are completed.

BACK: With smaller needles and royal blue, cast on 78 (84, 92) sts and work in k 1, p 1 ribbing for 2 inches; inc 1 st on last row—79 (85, 93) sts.

Change to larger needles and work even in st st to establish plaid pattern as follows: Work 9 rows with royal blue, 1 row with red, 2 rows with royal blue, 1 row with red, 9 rows with royal blue, 1 row with spruce, 2 rows with royal blue, 1 row with spruce, 9 rows with royal blue, 1 row with red, 2 rows with royal blue, 1 row with red, and 9 rows with royal blue.

Rep these 48 rows for plaid pat until total length measures 15 (15½, 15½) inches, or desired length to underarm, ending with a p row.

ARMHOLE SHAPING: Bind off 3 (3, 4) sts at beg of next 2 rows. Bind off 2 (2, 2) sts at beg of following 2 rows. Dec 1 st at each end every other row 6 (6, 6) times. Work even over rem 57 (63, 69) sts until length past beg of armholes measures 7½ (7½, 8) inches.

SHOULDER SHAPING: Bind off 5 (5, 6) sts at beg of next 4 (2, 6) rows. Bind off 6 (6, 0) sts at beg of next 2 (4, 0) rows. Sl rem 25 (29, 33) sts to holder for back of neck.

LEFT FRONT: With smaller needles and blue, cast on 36 (38, 42) sts. Work in k 1, p 1 ribbing for 2 inches, inc 0 (1, 1) sts on last row—36 (39, 43) sts. Change to larger needles. Work even in plaid pat until length to beg of armhole shaping equals that of Back, and same pat row as beg of armhole shaping as Back, ending with a p row.

ARMHOLE SHAPING: Bind off 3 (3, 4) sts at beg of next row. Work 1 row even. Bind off 2 (2, 2) sts at beg of next row, then dec 1 st at armhole edge every other row 6 (6, 6) times. Work even over rem 25 (28, 31) sts until length past beg of armholes measures 5½ (5½, 6) inches, ending with a p row.

NECK SHAPING: Work across first 20 (23, 24) sts, sl rem 5 (5, 7) sts to holder to be worked later. Working over the sts on needle only, dec 1 st at neck edge every other row 4 (6, 6) times—16 (17, 18) sts. Work even until length to shoulder shaping equals that of Back, ending at armhole edge.

SHOULDER SHAPING: *Row 1:* Bind off 5 (5, 6) sts; complete row.
*Row 2:* Work even.
*Row 3:* Rep Row 1.
*Row 4:* Work even. Bind off rem sts. Fasten off.

RIGHT FRONT: Work as for Left Front, reversing shaping.

SLEEVES: With smaller needles and royal blue, cast on 38 (40, 44) sts. Work k 1, p 1 ribbing for 3½ (3½, 4) inches, inc 5 (5, 7) sts on last row—43 (45, 51) sts. Change to larger needles. Work in plaid pat and *at same time,* inc 1 st each end every 8 (6, 6) rows until there are 61 (65, 71) sts. Work even until total length measures 16½ (17, 17½) inches, ending in same pat as beg of armhole shaping of Left Front and Back, ending with a p row.

TOP SHAPING: Bind off 3 (3, 3) sts at beg of next 4 rows. Dec 1 st each end every sixth row 6 (6, 6) times; then bind off 3 (3, 3) sts at beg of next 4 rows. *Next row:* (K 3 tog) across, ending with k 1 (2, 2). Bind off tightly.

BACK EMBROIDERY: Begin the vertical striping on the first stitch to the right of center st. Work duplicate st (see page 85) with spruce above the ribbing to top of Back. Working toward the right side of Back, (sk next 6 sts; with red, work duplicate st over next st to top of Back; sk next st to right, work red duplicate sts over next st to top of Back) twice; sk next 6 sts; with spruce, work duplicate st over next st to top; sk next st; with spruce, work duplicate st over next st to top. Continue in plaid pat as established, working toward right-side edge, then work toward left edge of Back to correspond.

SLEEVE EMBROIDERY: Mark center st. Work duplicate st pat same as for Back.

RIGHT FRONT EMBROIDERY: Working from center front to side seam, sk 4 sts at center Front, (with red, work duplicate st over next st; sk next st; with red, work duplicate st over next st; sk next 6 sts) twice; with spruce, work duplicate st over next st; sk next st, with spruce, work duplicate st over next st. Continue in plaid pat as established, working toward side edge. (*Note:* For Size Medium only, omit duplicate st at edge.)

LEFT FRONT EMBROIDERY: Work same as for Right Front, working from center front to side seam.

FINISHING: Pin pieces to measurements, dampen, and leave to dry. Sew shoulder seams; sew side and sleeve seams. Sew in sleeves.

LEFT FRONT BUTTONBAND: With right side facing, smaller needles, and blue, pick up and k 116 (120, 124) sts along center front edge. Work k 1, p 1 ribbing for 9 rows. Bind off in ribbing. Mark positions for 6 buttons having first button 1 inch above lower edge and last button evenly spaced below neck edge.

RIGHT FRONT BUTTONHOLE BAND: Work same as for Button Band through Row 4.
*Row 5:* Make buttonhole opposite each button mark as follows: Work in ribbing to first pin, * bind off next 2 sts, work in ribbing to next pin. Rep from * to last pin, bind off 2 sts, work to end.
*Row 6:* Work in ribbing, *and at same time,* cast on 2 sts over 2 bound off sts of previous row.
*Rows 7–9:* Work in ribbing; bind off as for Left Front Buttonband.

NECKBAND: With right side facing, smaller needles, and royal blue, begin at right neck edge; pick up 80 (86, 90) sts around entire neck edge, including sts on holders. Work k 1, p 1 ribbing for ½ inch. Work buttonhole in line with previous buttonholes over next 2 rows. Work even until ribbing measures same as Front bands. Bind off in ribbing. Sew on buttons.

## Man's Plaid Vest

Shown on page 27.
Directions are for size Medium (40–42). Chest measurement = 43 inches.

**MATERIALS**

Coats and Clark Royal Mouliné Knitting Worsted (50-gram balls): 7 balls No. 6001 red, 1 ball *each* of No. 6017 black and No. 6020 ecru
Sizes 6 and 9 knitting needles, or size to obtain gauge below.
2 stitch holders
Safety pin
Blunt end tapestry needle

**Abbreviations:** Page 217.
**Gauge:** With larger needles over st st, 9 sts = 2 inches; 13 rows = 2 inches.

**INSTRUCTIONS**

BACK: With smaller needles, and black, cast on 92 sts and work in k 1, p 1 ribbing for 2 inches; inc 4 sts on last row—96 sts.

Change to larger needles and st st (k 1 row, p 1 row) working even until total length measures 15 inches or desired length to underarm, ending with p row.

ARMHOLE SHAPING: Bind off 6 sts at beg of next 2 rows. Dec 1 st each side every other row 4 times—76 sts. Work even on rem 76 sts until length from beg of armhole shaping measures 10 inches, ending with p row.

SHOULDER SHAPING: Bind off 8 sts at beg of next 4 rows. Bind off 7 sts at beg of next 2 rows. Sl rem 30 st to holder for Back neck.

FRONT: *Note:* Horizontal stripes are worked in stockinette stitch as you knit the sweater. The vertical stripes are worked in duplicate st when Front is completed.

Work as for Back to top of ribbing. Change to larger needles, st st, and work 8 rows with red. Begin to work plaid pat as follows: 1 row of black, 2 rows with red, 1 row with ecru, 2 rows with red, 1 row with black, 11 rows with red. Rep these 18 rows for plaid pat. Keeping to pat, work same as Back until piece measures same as back to Armhole Shaping, end with p row.

FIRST ARMHOLE AND NECK SHAPINGS: Bind off 6 sts, knit 41 sts; place next 2 sts on safety pin and rem 47 sts onto a stitch holder. Dec 1 st at arm edge every other row 4 times *and at the same time,* dec 1 st at neck edge every other row 14 times. Work even on rem 23 sts until same length as Back to Shoulder, end with p row.

FIRST SHOULDER SHAPING: Bind off 8 sts at arm edge twice. Bind off rem 7 sts at armhole edge.

SECOND ARMHOLE AND NECK SHAPING: Sl 47 sts from holder to needle and beg at armhole edge, bind off 6 sts, k 41 sts and work ARMHOLE, NECK, and SHOULDER SHAPINGS to correspond with opposite side.

EMBROIDERY: With right side facing, working from right edge of Front and working toward left edge, and beginning above the ribbing, embroider in duplicate stitches (see page 85 for how-to) as follows: sk 13 sts from side edge, (work stripe of duplicate sts with black in next st to top of Front; sk 2 sts, work stripe of duplicate sts with ecru; sk 2 sts, work stripe of duplicate sts with black; sk 13 sts) 4 times.

NECKBAND: Sew left shoulder seam. With right side facing, smaller needles, and black, knit across 30 sts on Back holder; pick up 64 sts along left neckline edge, k 2 sts on safety pin, placing a st marker on needle between these 2 sts; pick up 64 sts along right neckline edge—160 sts. Work in k 1 p 1 ribbing to 1 st before marker, p 2, work in k 1, p 1 ribbing to the end of the row.

*Next row* (decrease row): Work in ribbing as established to 2 sts before marker, k 2 tog, sl 1, k 1, psso; work in ribbing to end of row.

Working in ribbing, rep decrease row every other row two times more. Work 1 row even after last decrease row. Bind off in ribbing.

ARMBAND: Sew right shoulder and neckband seam. With right side facing, smaller needles, and black, pick up 112 sts around armhole edge. Work in ribbing for 7 rows; bind off in ribbing. Sew side seams and block to finish.

## Child's Plaid Crew Neck Pullover

Shown on page 26.
Instructions are for Size Small (4-6); changes for Size Medium (8-10) and Size Large (12) follow in parentheses. Finished chest = 27½ (30, 33) inches.

**MATERIALS**

Coats & Clark Royal Mouliné worsted wool (50-gram balls), or a suitable substitute, in the following amounts and colors: 6 (7, 8) balls of No. 6005 lemon yellow, 1 ball *each* of No. 6017 black and No. 6001 red
Sizes 5 and 9 knitting needles, or size to obtain gauge given below

**Abbreviations:** Page 217.
**Gauge:** With larger needles over st st, 9 sts = 2 inches; 13 rows = 2 inches.

**INSTRUCTIONS**

BACK: With smaller needles and lemon, cast on 62 (68, 74) sts. Work k 1, p 1 ribbing for 1½ (1½, 2) inches. Change to larger needles and st st. Work even until total length measures 10 (12, 13) inches.

ARMHOLE SHAPING: Bind off 3 (3, 3) sts at beg of next 2 rows. Bind off 2 (2, 2) sts at beg of following 2 rows. Dec 1 st at each end every other row 5 (6, 7) times. Work even over rem 42 (46, 50) sts until length past beg of armholes measures 6 (6½, 7) inches.

SHOULDER SHAPING: Bind off 4 (4, 5) sts at beg of next 6 (4, 6) rows. Bind off 0 (5, 0) sts at beg of next 0 (2, 0) rows. Sl rem 18 (20, 20) sts to holder for back of neck.

FRONT: Work as for Back until ribbing has been completed, inc 1 st at end of last row worked—63 (69, 75) sts. Change to larger needles and st st. *Note:* Horizontal stripes are worked in st st as you knit the sweater. The vertical stripes are worked in duplicate st after Front is completed.

PLAID PAT: Work stripe sequence for all sizes as follows: 9 rows lemon, 1 row red, 1 row lemon, 1 row black, 1 row lemon, 1 row red. Rep these 14 rows for plaid pat.

ARMHOLE SHAPING: Work same as for Back until length past beg of armhole shaping measures 4½ (5, 5) inches, ending with a wrong-side row.

NECK SHAPING: Work across first 15 (16, 18) sts. Sl rem 28 (31, 33) sts to holder to be worked later. Working over the sts on needle for left shoulder, dec 1 st at neck edge every other row 3 (3, 3) times. Work even until length to shoulder shaping equals that of Back, ending at armhole edge.

LEFT SHOULDER SHAPING: *Row 1:* Bind off 4 (4, 5) sts; complete row.

*Row 2:* Work even.

*Row 3:* Bind off 4 (4, 5) sts; complete row.

*Row 4:* Work even. Bind off the rem sts.

RIGHT SHOULDER: Leaving center 13 (15, 15) sts on holder to be worked later, sl rem 15 (16, 18) sts to needle. Attach yarn at neck edge and work right shoulder as for left, reversing shaping.

SLEEVES: With smaller needles and lemon, cast on 30 (32, 34) sts. Work k 1, p 1 ribbing for 1½ (1½, 2) inches, inc 6 (6, 6) sts on last row—36 (38, 40) sts.

Change to larger needles and st st, inc 1 st at each end every 8th (8th, 8th) row until there are 48 (52, 56) sts on needle. Work even until total length measures 12 (14, 15) inches, ending with a p row.

TOP SHAPING: Bind off 3 (3, 3) sts at beg of next 2 rows. Bind off 2 sts at beg of next 4 rows. Dec 1 st at each end of every other row 5 (6, 7) times. Bind off 2 sts at beg of next 4 rows and 3 sts at beg of next 2 (2, 2) rows. Bind off rem 10 (12, 14) sts.

FRONT EMBROIDERY: *Vertical stripes:* Mark center front st. Beg above ribbing with black, work duplicate st over center st to top of Front. Sk next st to right of center; with red, work duplicate st over next st to top of Front. Sk next 8 (8, 8) sts. With red, work duplicate st over next st to top of Front. Sk next st. With black, work duplicate st over next st to top of Front. Sk next st. With red, work duplicate st over next st to top of Front. Continue in plaid pat as established, working to right side edge, then work left half of Front in same manner.

NECKBAND: Sew right shoulder seam. With right side facing, smaller needles, and lemon, pick up 58 (62, 64) sts around entire neck edge, including sts on holder. Work k 1, p 1 ribbing for 1¼ (1¼, 1½) inches. Bind off in ribbing.

FINISHING: Sew left shoulder, neckband, side, and sleeve seams. Sew in sleeves. Pin pieces out to measurements, dampen, and leave to dry. Fold neckband in half to right side; hem in place.

## Knitting Plaids

To knit mock plaids, work the blocks in stockinette stitch using two strands of sport-weight yarn.

For example, to simulate a blackwatch plaid, knit two strands of green or blue held together to create the solid green or solid blue blocks. Knit strands of green (or blue) and black held together to create the more subtly colored bands found in the design. Carry bobbins to ease the color changes across the rows.

Create the narrow stripes in the plaid using duplicate stitch worked vertically and horizontally atop the knitted fabric, as shown below.

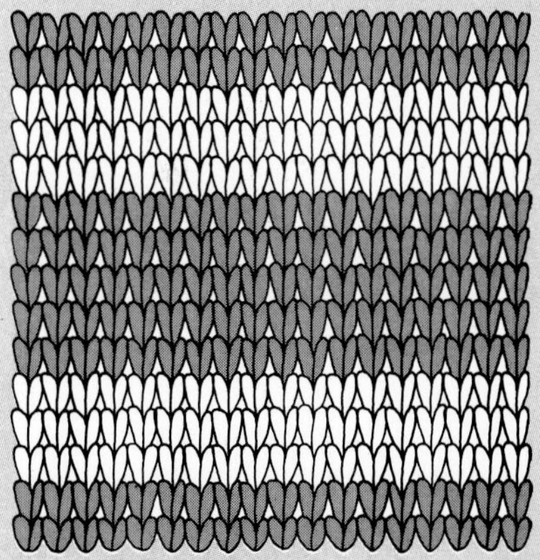

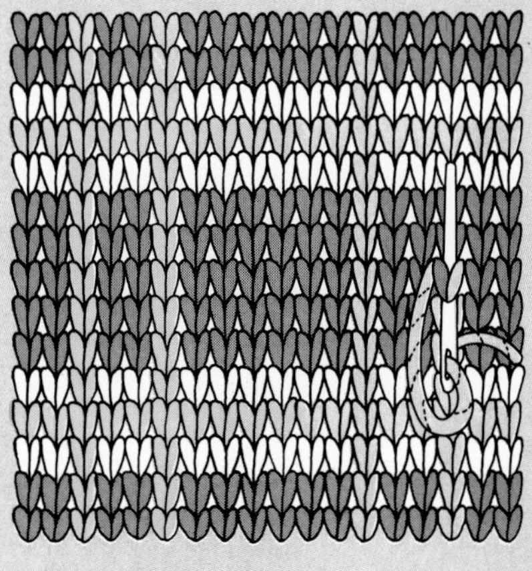

*A Celebration of Color, Pattern, and Texture*

# EXPLORING TEXTURE

***Knitting and crocheting to create interesting textures is a happy combination of material and technique. Many textures are the result of specialty stitches for both overall patterns and isolated texture elements. At other times you can create wonderful effects using simple stitches worked with a spectacular yarn.***

Centuries of traditional fisherman knitting have resulted in a wealth of texture patterns. The wool rug at *left* is a sampler of favorites, including a diamond repeat pattern filled in with panels of seed stitch and flanked by a simple cable and a Tree of Life design. Bands of garter stitch are used to edge the rug and to help keep it flat.

Instructions for projects shown in this chapter begin on page 44.

# EXPLORING TEXTURE

Traditional fisherman knitting is a centuries-old cottage industry from the British Isles. Worked in lanolin-rich, undyed hand-spun wool, fisherman-knit sweaters are naturally water-resistant. This quality makes them excellent for wearing at sea.

Each locale has become known for its own distinctive patterns, and, like tartans, the patterns can be linked to individual families or clans. Islands such as Guernsey, Jersey, and the Arans not only have identifiable stitch patterns, but distinctive garment construction details.

The stitches themselves take their names from everyday life in the seaside regions. Ropes on fishing boats perhaps inspired cables; winding paths up rocky hills resemble knitted zigzags. Other patterns such as ladder, spoon, and waffle stitches closely mimic their real-life counterparts.

The woman's pullover *opposite* is an example of classic fisherman knitting. A center panel on the pullover, which is adjusted in width for each size, is worked in a waffle stitch, and symmetrically flanked by a variety of other textured stitches.

Also knit the matching cap, *above,* for a chilly autumn day. Begin with a double-cable strip to form the brim. Then pick up stitches along one long edge to form the crown.

These fisherman-knit designs are worked in a soft berry color; for a more traditional look, work them in a natural color such as eggshell or beige. Unscoured wool, which is spun in ways that help retain natural lanolin, is available from most yarn shops to create knitted outerwear that is water-resistant.

# EXPLORING TEXTURE

A fun way to learn to work with knitted and crocheted texture stitches is to make a sampler.

For example, you might try working up several same-size swatches from your leftover yarns into various types of texture stitches. Then assemble them to make a one-of-a-kind afghan or throw.

Or, you might approach texture from a different viewpoint, and work one or two texture pattern stitches in an interesting assortment of yarns, including nubby wools, sleek cottons, or fuzzy mohair blends.

The two women's pullovers, *opposite,* are identically styled, but one is knitted and the other is crocheted. The crocheted sampler pullover, *near right,* features twelve squares with four different texture patterns. The knitted version, *far right,* is made similarly. Both sweaters feature plain crocheted or knitted backs and sleeves.

For added effect, the sweaters are worked with two strands of yarn held together. Color contrasts between the strands result in a tweedy look. Because each of the texture samples is worked individually, you can take the work with you and craft on the go.

# EXPLORING TEXTURE

Of all the knitted stitches, cross-overs—or cables—afford the widest variety of texture stitch possibilities.

A sequence of rows of cable twists, each properly spaced and twisted to the right or left, results in the lattice-look stitch on the place mats, *above.* These sunny yellow place mats are worked in a thick cotton yarn; a trim crocheted edging keeps them lying flat.

Five distinctive crochet patterns are repeated in the runner, *opposite.* Worked in creamy rug wool, the runner features 15 bands of textured crochet separated by two rows of single crochet worked in contrasting colors.

The stitches used include a blackberry stitch, simple shells, and variations of stitches worked in front and back loops of stitches from the previous row.

## Knitted Aran Rug

Shown on pages 36–37.
Finished size is 22x31 inches, excluding fringe.

**MATERIALS**
Paternayan Rug Yarn (62-yard skeins): 8 skeins of off-white
Size 10½ circular 29-inch knitting needle
Size I crochet hook
Stitch markers

**Abbreviations:** Page 217.
**Gauge:** 10 st sts = 3 inches.

**INSTRUCTIONS**
PATTERN 1: Garter stitch over 4 stitches.
Knit every row.

PATTERN 2: Seed stitch over 5 stitches.
*Row 1:* * K 1, p 1; rep from * once more, k 1.
Rep Row 1 for pat.

PATTERN 3: Tree of Life over 9 stitches.
*Row 1* (right side): P 3, k 3 through the back loop—TBL, p 3.
*Row 2:* K 3, p 3 TBL, k 3.
*Row 3:* P 2; sl next st to cable needle and hold in *back* of work; k 1 TBL, p 1 from cable needle, k 1 TBL; sl next st to cable needle and hold in *front* of work, p 1, k 1 TBL from cable needle, p 2.
*Row 4:* K 2, p 1 TBL, k 1, p 1 TBL, k 1, p 1 TBL, k 2.
*Row 5:* P 1; sl next st to cable needle and hold in *back* of work, k 1 TBL, p 1 from cable needle, p 1, k 1 TBL, p 1; sl next st to cable needle and hold in *front* of work, p 1, k 1 TBL from cable needle, p 1.
*Row 6:* K 1, p 1 TBL, k 2, p 1 TBL, k 2, p 1 TBL, k 1.
*Row 7:* Sl next st to cable needle and hold in *back* of work, k 1 TBL, p 1 from cable needle, p 2, k 1 TBL, p 2; sl next st to cable needle and hold in *front* of work, p 1, k 1 TBL from cable needle.
*Row 8:* P 1 TBL, k 3, p 1 TBL, k 3, p 1 TBL.
Rep these 8 rows for Tree of Life pat.

PATTERN 4: Cable pat over 7 sts.
*Row 1:* K 6, p 1 on right side of center; p 1, k 6 on left side of center.
*Row 2:* P 6, k 1 on right side of center; k 1, p 6 on left side of center.
*Row 3:* Rep Row 1.
*Row 4:* Rep Row 2.
*Row 5: On right side of center,* sl 3 sts to cable needle and hold in *back* of work, k 3, k 3 from cable needle, p 1. *On left side of center,* p 1, sl 3 sts to cable needle and hold in *back* of work, k 3, k 3 from cable needle.
*Row 6:* P 6, k 1 on right side of center; k 1, p 6 on left side of center.
*Row 7:* K 6, p 1 on right side of center; p 1, k 6 on left side of center.
*Row 8:* P 6, k 1 on right side of center; k 1, p 6 on left side of center.
Rep these 8 rows for cable pat.

PATTERN 5: Zigzag stitch worked over 1 st.
*Row 1:* Inc 1 st by knitting into st below, k 1, sl inc over k 1.
*Row 2:* Pick up 2 slanted lps at base of next st and sl back onto left-hand needle; p 2 picked-up sts tog, p 1, sl first st over second stitch.
*Row 3:* Pick up 2 slanted lps at base of next st and sl back onto left-hand needle and knit as one st; k 1, sl first st over last st.
Rep Rows 2–3 for zigzag pat.

PATTERN 6: Diamond pat worked over 19 sts.
*Row 1:* P 7; sl next 2 sts to cable needle and hold in *front,* k 2 TBL, p 1, k 2 TBL from cable needle; p 7.
*Row 2:* K 7, p 2, k 1, p 2, k 7.
*Row 3:* P 6; sl next st to cable needle and hold in *back,* k 2 TBL, p 1 from cable needle, k 1, sl next 2 sts to cable needle and hold in *front,* p 1, k 2 TBL from cable needle; p 6.
*Row 4:* K 6, p 2, k 1, p 1, k 1, p 2, k 6.
*Row 5:* P 5; sl next st to cable needle and hold in *back,* k 2 TBL, p 1 from cable needle, k 1, p 1, k 1, sl next 2 sts to cable needle and hold in *front,* p 1, k 2 TBL from cable needle; p 5.
*Row 6:* K 5, p 2, k 1, p 1, k 1, p 1, k 1, p 2, k 5.
*Row 7:* P 4; sl next st to cable needle and hold in *back,* k 2 TBL, p 1 from cable needle; (k 1, p 1) 3 times, k 1; sl next 2 sts to cable needle and hold in *front,* p 1, k 2 TBL from cable needle; p 4.
*Row 8:* K the k sts, p the p sts.
*Row 9:* P 3; sl next st to cable needle and hold in *back,* k 2 TBL, p 1 from cable needle; (k 1, p 1) 3 times, k 1; sl next 2 sts to cable needle and hold in *front,* p 1, k 2 TBL from cable needle; p 3.
*Row 10:* K the k sts, p the p sts.
*Row 11:* P 2; sl next st to cable needle and hold in *back,* k 2 TBL, p 1 from cable needle; (k 1, p 1) 4 times, k 1; sl next 2 sts to cable needle and hold in *front,* p 1, k 2 TBL from cable needle; p 2.
*Row 12:* K the k sts, p the p sts.
*Row 13:* P 1; sl next st to cable needle and hold in *back,* k 2 TBL, p 1 from cable needle; (k 1, p 1) 5 times, k 1; sl next 2 sts to cable needle and hold in *front,* p 1, k 2 TBL from cable needle; p 1.
*Row 14:* K the k sts, p the p sts.
*Row 15:* P 1; sl 2 sts to cable needle and hold in *front,* p 1, k 2 TBL from cable needle; (p 1, k 1) 5 times, p 1; sl next st to cable needle and hold in *back,* k 2 TBL, p 1 from cable needle; p 1.
*Row 16 and all even-numbered rows:* Rep Row 14.

*Row 17:* P 2; sl 2 sts to cable needle and hold in *front,* p 1, k 2 TBL from cable needle; (p 1, k 1) 4 times, p 1; sl next st to cable needle and hold in *back,* k 2 TBL, p 1 from cable needle; p 2.

*Row 19:* P 3; sl 2 sts to cable needle and hold in *front,* p 1, k 2 TBL from cable needle; (p 1, k 1) 3 times, p 1; sl next st to cable needle and hold in *back,* k 2 TBL, p 1 from cable needle; p 3.

*Row 21:* P 4; sl 2 sts to cable needle and hold in *front,* p 1, k 2 TBL from cable needle; (p 1, k 1) 2 times, p 1; sl next st to cable needle and hold in *back,* k 2 TBL, p 1 from cable needle; p 4.

*Row 23:* P 5; sl 2 sts to cable needle and hold in *front,* p 1, k 2 TBL from cable needle; (p 1, k 1) once, p 1; sl next st to cable needle and hold in *back,* k 2 TBL, p 1 from cable needle; p 5.

*Row 25:* P 6; sl next 2 sts to cable needle and hold in *front,* p 1, k 2 TBL from cable needle, p 1; sl next st to cable needle and hold in *back,* k 2 TBL, p 1 from cable needle; p 6.

RUG: With Size 10½ knitting needle cast on 71 stitches. Knit 8 rows for border.

FOUNDATION ROW: *Note:* Place stitch markers bet pat stitches and carry along as you work for ease in knitting.

Working over the 71 sts, establish pat as follows: 4 sts Pat 1; 5 sts Pat 2; 9 sts Pat 3; 7 sts Pat 4; 1 st Pat 5; 19 sts Pat 6; 1 st Pat 5; 7 sts Pat 4; 9 sts Pat 3; 5 sts Pat 2; 4 sts Pat 1.

Follow directions for each pat until 5 diamonds are completed, ending with Row 1 of diamond pat. Knit 8 rows, binding off on the ninth row.

FRINGE: Cut 12-inch lengths of yarn, fold in half. With crochet hook pull 1 strand of yarn through each st along both ends of rug and knot in place. In bundles of 4 strands of yarn, tie knots (8 ends). Trim ends.

# Irish Knit Pullover and Hat

Shown on pages 38–39.

Directions are for Size Petite (6); changes for Sizes Small (8–10), Medium (12–14), and Large (16) follow in parentheses. Bust = 34 (36, 38, 40) inches. Finished size for head is 21–23 inches.

**MATERIALS**

**For the sweater**

Ultex Rustic (50-gram balls): 14 (14, 15, 15) balls No. 6039 cranberry

Sizes 5 and 7 knitting needles or size to obtain gauge given below

16-inch circular needle, Size 7

**For the hat**

Ultex Rustic (50-gram balls): 3 balls No. 6039 cranberry

Size 6 double-pointed needles or size to obtain gauge given below

Size H aluminum crochet hook

Stitch markers

**Abbreviations:** Page 217.

**Gauge:** For the sweater, with larger needles over double moss st, 4 sts = 1 inch.

For the hat, over waffle st, 5 sts = 1 inch.

**INSTRUCTIONS**

DOUBLE MOSS ST: (worked over 10 sts)

*Rows 1 and 4:* (K 2, p 2) twice, k 2.

*Rows 2 and 3:* (P 2, k 2) twice, p 2. Rep these 4 rows for pat.

SINGLE RIB ST: (worked over 1 st) *Row 1:* K 1 in row below.

*Row 2:* Purl. Rep these 2 rows for pat.

LADDER ST: (worked over 5 sts)

*Rows 1, 3, 5, 7, and 8:* Knit.

*Rows 2, 4, and 6:* Purl. Rep these 8 rows for pat.

ZIGZAG ST: (worked over 1 st)

*Row 1:* Inc 1 st by knitting into the st below, k 1, sl inc over k 1.

*Row 2:* Pick up 2 slanted lps at base on next st and sl back onto left-hand needle, p 2 picked-up sts tog; p 1, sl first st over second st.

*Row 3:* Pick up 2 slanted lps at base of next st, sl these back onto left-hand needle and k as one st; k 1, sl first st over last st.

Rep Rows 2–3 for pat.

SPOON ST: (worked over 8 sts)

*Row 1:* K 8.

*Rows 2 and 10:* P 8.

*Row 3:* Sl 2 sts to cable needle and hold in *back* of work, k 2; p 2 from cable needle, sl 2 sts to cable needle and hold in *front* of work, k 2; p 2 from cable needle.

*Rows 4, 6, and 8:* P 2, k 4, p 2.

*Rows 5 and 7:* K 2, p 4, k 2.

*Row 9:* Sl 2 sts to cable needle and hold in *front* of work, k 2, k 2 from cable needle, sl 2 sts to cable needle and hold in *back* of work, k 2, k 2 from cable needle. Rep these 10 rows for pat.

CABLE ST: (worked over 6 sts)

*Rows 1 and 5:* Knit.

*Rows 2, 4, and 6:* Purl.

*Row 3:* Sl 3 sts to cable needle and hold in *back* of work, k 3, k 3 from cable needle.

Rep these 6 rows for pat.

WAFFLE ST: (worked over an even number of sts)

*Row 1:* * Yo, k 2, sl yo over k 2 and off needle; rep from * across.

*Row 2:* Purl. Rep these 2 rows for pat. *Note:* When working waffle st in rnds on cap, Rnd 1 is worked as Row 1 above, Rnd 2 is knit.

BACK: With smaller needles cast on 95 (99, 105, 109) sts.

*Row 1:* * K 1 through back lp—TBL, p 1; rep from * across, end k 1 TBL.

*Row 2:* * P 1 TBL, k 1; rep from * across, end p 1 TBL. Rep these 2 rows for 2 inches, inc 1 st on last row—96 (100, 106, 110) sts. Change to larger needles; pattern sts are worked in following order

*continued*

from right to left and are separated by single purl sts: double moss, single rib, ladder, zigzag, spoon, zigzag, cable, waffle, cable, zigzag, spoon, zigzag, ladder, single rib, double moss.

First two rows of combined pat sts are worked as follows: *Row 1:* (K 2, p 2) twice, k 2, k 1 in row below, place marker, p 1, place marker, k 5, place marker, p 1, place marker, [inc 1 by k into st below, k 1, sl inc over k 1], place marker, p 1, place marker, k 8, place marker, p 1, place marker; rep bet [ ]s; place marker, p 1, place marker, k 6, place marker, p 1, place marker, * yo, k 2, sl yo over k 2 and off needle. Rep from * 9 (11, 14, 16) times, place marker, p 1, place marker, k 6, place marker, p 1, place marker; rep bet [ ]s; place marker, p 1, place marker, k 8, place marker, p 1, place marker; rep bet [ ]s; place marker, p 1, place marker, k 5, place marker, p 1, place marker, k 1 in row below, k 2, (p 2, k 2) twice.

*Row 2:* Slipping markers as you come to them, (p 2, k 2) twice, p 3, k 1, p 5, k 1; [pick up 2 slanted lps at base on next st and sl back onto left-hand needle, p 2 picked-up sts tog; p 1, pass first st over second st]; k 1, p 8, k 1; rep bet [ ]s. K 1, p 6, k 1, p 20 (24, 30, 34), k 1, p 6, k 1; rep bet [ ]s. K 1, p 8, k 1; rep bet [ ]s. K 1, p 5, k 1, p 3, (k 2, p 2) twice.

Continue with Row 3 in patterns as established, purling single sts bet markers on right side and knitting them on wrong side; work even until total length measures 15 (15, 15½, 15½) inches, ending with wrong-side row.

ARMHOLE SHAPING: Bind off 6 (6, 7, 7) sts at beg of next 2 rows. Dec 1 st each end every other row 5 (6, 7, 7) times—74 (76, 78, 82) sts. Work even in pat until length from beg of armhole shaping measures 7 (7½, 8, 8) inches, ending with wrong-side row.

SHOULDER SHAPING: Bind off 5 (5, 5, 6) sts at beg of next 6 rows, bind off 6 (6, 7, 5) sts at beg of next 2 rows. Sl rem 32 (34, 34, 36) sts to holder for Back neck.

FRONT: Work as for Back until length from beg of armhole shaping measures 5 (5½, 6, 6) inches, ending with a wrong-side row.

NECK SHAPING: Work 29 (29, 29, 31) sts. Join second ball and bind off next 16 (18, 20, 20) sts for Front neck. Work across rem 29 (29, 29, 31) sts for Right Front. Working both sides at once, bind off 3 sts 1 (1, 1, 1) time at neck edge, 2 sts at neck edge 1 (1, 1, 1) time, then dec 1 st at neck edge 3 (3, 2, 3) times—21 (21, 22, 23) sts. *At the same time,* when armhole is same length as Back to shoulder, shape shoulder as for Back.

SLEEVE: With smaller needles cast on 40 (42, 42, 42) sts. Work in ribbing as for Back for 15 rows. Inc 4 sts spaced evenly on last row—44 (46, 46, 46) sts.

Change to larger needles. Pattern sts are worked in following order from right to left and are separated by single purl sts: double moss, cable, zigzag, spoon, zigzag, cable, double moss. First two rows of combined pat sts are worked as follows:

*Row 1:* K 0 (1, 1, 1), (p 2, k 2) twice, place marker, p 1, place marker, k 6, place marker, p 1, place marker, [inc 1 by k into st below, k 1, sl inc over k 1], place marker, p 1, place marker, k 8, place marker, p 1, place marker, rep bet [ ]s, place marker, p 1, place marker, k 6, place marker, p 1, place marker, (k 2, p 2) twice, k 0 (1, 1, 1).

*Row 2:* Slipping markers as you come to them, p 0 (1, 1, 1), (k 2, p 2) twice, k 1, p 6, k 1, [insert right needle from right to left into 2 slanted lps at base of next st, insert left needle from right to left into same lps, remove right needle, p these 2 lps tog, p 1, pass first st over second st], k 1, p 8, k 1. Rep bet [ ]s, k 1, p 6, k 1, (p 2, k 2) twice, p 0 (1, 1, 1).

Continue with Row 3 in pats as established, inc 1 st each edge every fourth row to 74 (74, 80, 80) sts, working increased sts in double moss st. Work even until total length measures 17 (17½, 18, 18½) inches, ending with wrong-side row.

ARMHOLE SHAPING: Bind off 6 (6, 6, 6) sts at beg of next 2 rows, bind off 2 sts at beg of next 10 (10, 12, 12) rows. Dec 1 st at each end every right-side row 5 (5, 5, 5) times. *Next row* (wrong side): Work even. Bind off 10 sts at beg of next 2 rows. Bind off rem 12 (12, 14, 14) sts.

FINISHING: Weave shoulder seams and steam seam lightly. With right side facing and smaller circular needle, beginning at right shoulder, work 32 (34, 34, 36) sts from Back neck holder, pick up 15 (17, 20, 20) sts along left neck edge, pick up 16 (18, 20, 20) sts from Front neck, pick up 15 (17, 20, 20) sts along right neck edge—78 (86, 94, 96) sts. Join and work (k 1 TBL, p 1) ribbing for 15 rnds. Bind off loosely, fold to inside, and stitch down loosely. Sew sleeve and side seams, set in sleeves. Steam seams and entire sweater lightly.

HAT: (*Note:* See pullover, *above,* for stitch instructions.)

Cast on 21 sts on one needle. Pat sts are worked in the following order from right to left and they are separated by single purl sts: zigzag, spoon, zigzag, and cable. Working back and forth with two needles, work first two rows of combined pat sts as follows:

*Row 1* (foundation row): P 1, place marker, [inc by k into st below, k 1, sl inc over k 1], place marker, p 1, place marker, k 8, place marker, p 1, place marker, rep bet [ ]s, place marker, p 1, place marker, k 6, place marker, p 1.

*Row 2:* Slipping markers as you come to them, k 1, p 6, k 1, [pick up 2 slanted lps at base on next st and sl back onto left-hand needle, p 2 picked-up sts tog; p 1, pass first st over second st]; k 1, p 8, k 1, rep bet [ ]s, k 1.

Continue with Row 3 of pat sts purling single sts at edges and between markers on right-side rows and knitting them on wrong-side rows until total length measures 20 inches. Bind off. Seam bound-off edge to cast-on edge. With three double-pointed needles pick up 128 sts around cable edge and join.

Knit 1 round.

*Rnd 1:* * Yo, k 2, pass yo over k 2; rep from * around.

*Rnd 2:* * K 16, place marker; rep from * around. Hat is divided into 8 sections.

Rep Rnds 1–2, slipping markers 7 times more.

*Rnd 17:* Rep Rnd 1.

*Rnd 18:* K around, k 2 tog after each marker.

*Rnd 19:* Work in pat, dec in pat after each marker as follows: [Yo, k 2 tog, k 1, pass yo over 2 sts, * yo, k 2, pass yo over 2 sts; rep from * to next marker]; rep bet [ ]s around.

Rep Rnds 18–19 until 8 sts total rem. Break off, draw end through rem 8 sts, draw tightly and fasten securely. Make pom-pom and attach to top of hat. With crochet hook, work 1 rnd reverse sc around lower edge of cap.

# Knitted Patchwork Pullover

Shown on pages 40–41.

Directions are for Size Small (8–10); changes for Size Medium (12–14) follow in parentheses. Finished bust measurement = 36 (39¼) inches.

**MATERIALS**

Coats & Clark Red Heart Sport Yarn: 14 (16) ounces No. 328 new camel; 2 ounces *each* of No. 845 royal blue, No. 920 cranberry, No. 666 bottle green, and No. 602 dark gold for each size

Sizes 6 and 8 knitting needles for Size Small; Sizes 7 and 9 for Size Medium, or sizes to obtain gauge given below

Cable needle

**Abbreviations:** Page 217.

**Gauge:** With 2 strands of yarn held tog and larger needles over st st for Size Small, 17 sts = 4 inches; 6 rows = 1 inch. With 2 strands of yarn held tog and larger needles over st st for Size Medium, 4 sts = 1 inch; 6 rows = 1 inch.

**INSTRUCTIONS**

*Note:* Garment is worked with 2 strands of yarn held together throughout.

BACK AND SIDE FRONT PANELS: Beg at lower edge with smaller needles and 2 strands of camel held tog, cast on 86 (90) sts. Work in k 1, p 1 ribbing for 3 inches, inc 1 st at end of last row—87 (91) sts. Change to larger needles and work in st st until total length measures 14 (14½) inches, ending with a p row.

RIGHT FRONT ARMHOLE SHAPING: *Row 1:* K 3, turn.

*Row 2:* P 3, turn.

*Row 3:* K 1, k 2 tog, turn.

*Row 4:* P 2, turn.

*Row 5:* K 2 tog, turn, p rem st. Fasten off.

With right side facing and using double strand, bind off next 8 (9) sts (1 st rem on right needle); k 64 (66), bind off next 8 (9) sts, k rem sts.

LEFT FRONT ARMHOLE SHAPING: *Row 1:* P 3, turn.

*Row 2:* K 2 tog, k 1, turn.

*Row 3:* P 2, turn.

*Row 4:* K 2 tog, turn, p rem st. Fasten off.

BACK ARMHOLE SHAPING: With wrong side facing, using double strand and beg with a p row, work 1 row even. Continue in st st, dec 1 st at each end on next row and every other row until 59 (61) sts rem. Work even until length past beg of armhole measures 7 (7½) inches, ending with a p row.

NECK SHAPING: *Row 1:* K first 21 (22) sts, sl rem sts to a holder; turn. Working over sts on needle only, dec 1 st at neck edge on next row and at same edge every other row until 18 (19) sts rem. Bind off.

Sl sts from holder onto needle and join yarn at neck edge.

*Row 1:* Bind off first 17 sts for center back, k rem 21 (22) sts; turn. Complete to correspond to other side.

FRONT RIBBING: With smaller needles and 2 strands of camel held tog, cast on 56 (58) sts. Work in k 1, p 1 ribbing for 3 inches. Bind off loosely in ribbing. Set aside.

SQUARE 1 (make 3): (*Note:* When changing colors, carry color not in use loosely along wrong side of work.)

With 2 strands of camel held tog and larger needles, cast on 22 sts.

*Rows 1–4:* Work in st st. At end of Row 4, join 2 strands of blue.

*Row 5:* (K 4 blue, k 2 camel) 3 times; k 4 blue.

*Row 6:* P 4 blue, (p 2 camel, p 4 blue) 3 times.

*Rows 7–8:* With camel only k 1 row, p 1 row.

*Row 9:* K 3 camel, (k 4 blue, k 2 camel) twice; k 4 blue, k 3 camel.

*Row 10:* P 3 camel, (p 4 blue, p 2 camel) twice; p 4 blue, p 3 camel.

*Rows 11–12:* Rep Rows 7–8.

*Rows 13–28:* Rep Rows 5–12 twice.

*Rows 29–32:* Rep Rows 5–8 once. Bind off.

SQUARE 2 (make 3): With 1 strand of camel and 1 strand of cranberry held tog, cast on 21 sts.

*continued*

*Row 1:* (K 3, p 3) 3 times; k 3.
*Row 2:* (P 3, k 3) 3 times; p 3.
*Rows 3–4:* Rep Row 1 twice.
*Rows 5–6:* Rep Rows 2 and 1.
*Rows 7–30:* Rep Rows 1–6 four times.
*Rows 31–32:* Rep Rows 1–2. Bind off.

SQUARE 3 (make 3): With 1 strand of camel and 1 strand of green held tog, cast on 22 sts.
*Row 1:* P 2, (k 2, p 2) 5 times.
*Row 2:* K 2, (p 2, k 2) 5 times.
*Row 3:* P 2, (sl next st to cable needle and hold in *front* of work, k 1, k st from cable needle; p 2) 5 times.
*Row 4:* Rep Row 2.
*Rows 5–32:* Rep Rows 1–4 seven times. Bind off.

SQUARE 4 (make 3): With 1 strand of camel and 1 strand of gold held tog, cast on 20 sts.
*Row 1:* (K 1, p 1) 10 times.
*Row 2:* (P 1, k 1) 10 times.
Rep last 2 rows alternately until 32 rows in all have been worked. Bind off.

Arrange the 12 squares for Front in 4 horizontal rows of 3 squares. Row 1 is the bottom row and, from left to right, is made of squares 2, 3, and 4. Row 2, from left to right, is made of squares 3, 4, and 1. Row 3, from left to right, is made of squares 4, 1, and 2. Row 4, from left to right, is made of squares 1, 2, and 3.

Sew squares tog, then sew top edge of Lower Ribbing to Front assembly, easing to fit.

SLEEVES: Beg at lower edge with smaller needles and 2 strands of camel held tog, cast on 40 (44) sts. Work in k 1, p 1 ribbing for 3 inches, inc 1 st at end of last row—41 (45) sts. Change to larger needles and work in st st for 1 inch, ending with a p row. Continuing in st st, inc 1 st at each side on next row and every eighth row until 57 (61) sts on needle. Work even until total length measures 16½ (17) inches, ending with a p row.

TOP SHAPING: Bind off 4 sts at beg of next 2 rows, dec 1 st at each side on next row and every fourth row until 43 (47) sts rem. Work 1 row even. Dec 1 st at each side on next row and every other row until 23 sts rem.

*Next row:* Purl. *Following row:* K 1, * k 2 tog. Rep from * across. Bind off.

Beg at lower edge of ribbing, sew long edge of each side panel to corresponding edge on front. (Extending front sections form upper armhole.)

For left shoulder seam, sew 18 (19) back shoulder sts to corresponding portion on front.

NECKBAND: With right side facing, smaller needles, and 2 strands of camel held tog, pick up and k 58 (60) sts along entire neck edge. Work in k 1, p 1 ribbing for 1 inch. Bind off loosely in ribbing.

Sew rem shoulder seam and sleeve seams; sew in sleeves.

## Crocheted Patchwork Pullover

Shown on pages 40–41.
Directions are for Size Small (8–10); changes for Size Medium (12–14) follow in parentheses. Bust = 34½ (38) inches.

**MATERIALS**
Coats & Clark Red Heart Sport Yarn: 18 ounces of No. 328 new camel; 2 ounces *each* of No. 602 dark gold, No. 666 bottle green, No. 920 cranberry, and No. 845 royal blue
Sizes F and H aluminum crochet hooks, or sizes to obtain gauge given below

**Abbreviations:** Page 211.
**Gauge:** With larger hook and 2 strands held tog, 3 hdc = 1 inch; 5 rows = 2 inches. With smaller hook and 2 strands held tog, each square measures 4½ inches wide and 4¼ inches long.

**INSTRUCTIONS**
*Note:* Garment is worked with 2 strands of yarn held tog. Lower and neck ribbing is worked after garment is completed.

BACK: Beg at lower edge above ribbing, with 2 strands of camel held tog, ch 64 (74).
*Row 1* (right side): Hdc in third ch from hook and in each ch across 63—(73) hdc, counting turning ch-2 at beg as hdc; ch 2, turn.
*Row 2:* Sk first st, hdc in next hdc and in each hdc across, hdc in top of ch-2; ch 2, turn.
Rep Row 2 until length measures 10 (9½) inches, mark for wrong side; ch 2, turn.

TOP SECTION, RIGHT FRONT EDGE AND ARMHOLE SHAPING: *Row 1:* Sk first hdc, hdc in next 3 (4) hdc; do not work over rem sts; ch 2, turn.
*Row 2:* Sk first hdc, **yo, draw up lp in each of next 2 hdc, yo and draw through 4 lps on hook—hdc dec made;** hdc in next 0 (1) hdc, hdc in top of ch-2—3 (4) hdc; ch 2, turn. *Row 3:* Sk first hdc, hdc in next 1 (2) hdc, hdc in top of ch-2; ch 2, turn.

Rep last row until total 18 (20) rows have been completed past beg of armhole shaping ending with a wrong-side row; fasten off.

TOP SECTION OF BACK AND ARMHOLE SHAPING: Sk next 4 (6) hdc on last long row worked. Join 2 strands camel to next hdc.

*Row 1:* Ch 2, hdc in next 46 (50) hdc; do not work over rem sts; ch 2, turn.

*Row 2:* Sk first hdc, dec 1 hdc over next 2 hdc, hdc in each hdc to last 2 sts, dec 1 hdc over last 2 sts—45 (49) hdc; ch 2, turn.

*Row 3:* Sk first hdc, hdc in next hdc and in each hdc across, hdc in top of ch-2; ch 2, turn.

Rep last row until length past first row of armhole shaping measures same as right Front, ending with a wrong-side row; ch 2, turn.

FIRST SHOULDER: *Row 1:* Sk first hdc, hdc in next 9 (10) hdc, do not work over rem sts; ch 2, turn.

*Row 2:* Sk first hdc, hdc in next hdc and in each st across; fasten off.

SECOND SHOULDER: With the right side facing, sk next 25 (27) hdc, join 2 strands camel to next hdc.

*Row 1:* Ch 2, hdc in rem 9 (10) hdc; ch 2, turn.

*Row 2:* Rep Row 2 of First Shoulder to complete.

TOP SECTION OF LEFT FRONT SIDE AND ARMHOLE SHAPING: With right side facing, sk next 4 (6) hdc on last long row worked, join 2 strands camel to next hdc.

*Row 1:* Ch 2, hdc in last 3 (4) hdc; ch 2, turn.

*Row 2:* Hdc in next 1 (2) hdc, dec 1 hdc over last 2 sts; ch 2, turn.

Beg with Row 3 of Right Front and Armhole Shaping, complete as for opposite side edge.

PATCHWORK PANEL: Crochet each square with smaller hook.

SQUARE 1 (make 3): With 1 strand gold and 1 strand camel held tog, ch 21 to measure 4½ inches.

*Row 1:* Dc in fourth ch from hook and in each ch across—19 dc, counting turning ch-3 at beg as 1 dc. Mark for right side; ch 1, turn.

*Row 2:* Sc in first dc and in each dc across, sc in top of ch-3; ch 1, turn.

*Row 3:* Sc in first sc, * **work dc around post, from front, of next dc 1 row below—foundation raised dc made;** sk sc behind raised dc just made, sc in next sc, sk the dc below the sc just made; rep from * across, ending with sc in last st—9 raised dc; ch 1, turn.

*Row 4:* Sc in each st across—19 sc; ch 1, turn.

*Row 5:* Sc in first sc, * **work dc around post, from front, of next raised dc 1 row below—raised dc over raised dc made;** sk sc behind raised dc just made, sc in next sc; rep from * across; ch 1, turn.

Rep Rows 4–5 for pat until total length measures 4¼ inches, ending with Row 4 of pat; fasten off.

SQUARE 2 (make 3): With 1 strand each of green and camel held tog, ch 20.

*Row 1:* **Holding back on hook last lp of each dc, make 3 dc in fourth ch from hook, yo, and draw through all lps on hook—cluster (cl) made;** * ch 1, sk 1 ch, cl in next ch; rep from * across—9 cl made. Mark for right side; ch 3, turn.

*Row 2:* * Cl in next ch-1 sp, ch 1; rep from * across, ending with cl in top of ch-3; ch 3, turn.

Rep last row for pat until total length measures 4¼ inches; fasten off.

SQUARE 3 (make 3): With 1 strand each of cranberry and camel held tog, ch 22.

*Row 1:* Dc in fourth ch from hook and in each ch across—20 dc, counting ch-3 as 1 dc; ch 3, turn.

*Rows 2–3:* Sk first dc, * **work dc around post, from back, of next dc—back raised dc made.** Work back raised dc around post of next 2 dc; **work dc around post, from front, of next dc—front raised dc made;** work front raised dc around post of next 2 dc; rep from * across, ending with dc in top of ch-3. Mark Row 2 for right side; ch 3, turn.

*Rows 4–5:* Sk first dc, * work front raised dc around post of next 3 dc, back raised dc around post of next 3 dc; rep from * across, dc in top of ch-3; ch 3, turn.

Rep Rows 2–5 for pat until total length is 4¼ inches; fasten off.

SQUARE 4 (make 3): With 2 strands of camel held tog, ch 21.

*Row 1:* Sc in second ch from hook and in each ch across—20 sc; ch 1, turn.

*Row 2:* Sc in first 3 sc, * **draw up lp in next sc, drop camel, with 2 strands of blue held tog, yo, draw through 2 lps on hook—color change made;** carrying camel along top of sts, with blue sc in next 3 sc, change to camel in next sc; with camel sc in next 3 sc, change to blue in next st; with blue sc in next 3 sc, change to camel in next st; with camel sc in last 4 sc. Mark for right side; ch 1, turn.

*Rows 3–5:* Rep Row 2. At end of last row, change from camel to blue; ch 1, turn.

*Rows 6–9:* With blue, sc in first 3 sc, change to camel in next sc, with camel sc in next 3 sc, change to blue in next sc; with blue sc in next 3 sc, change to camel in next sc; with camel sc in next 3 sc, change to blue; with blue sc in last 4 sc; ch 1, turn. In last st of Row 9 change to camel, ch 1, turn; rep Rows 2–9 until length is 4¼ inches; fasten off.

Arrange the 12 squares for Front in 4 horizontal rows of 3 squares. Row 1 is the bottom row and, from left to right, is made of squares 3, 2, and 1. Row 2, from left to right, is made of squares 2, 1, and 4. Row 3, from left to right, is made of squares 1, 4, and 3. Row 4, from left to right, is squares 4, 3, and 2.

*continued*

Being careful to have right sides facing, sew squares tog to form Front. Sew side edges of Front to corresponding edges of body and side front sections easing latter to fit. At top edge place markers 3 (3½) inches in from each armhole edge.

FIRST SHOULDER: With right side of Front facing and using larger hook, join 2 strands camel to end st at top of left shoulder.

*Row 1:* Ch 2, make 9 (10) hdc across to first marker; ch 2, turn.

*Row 2:* Sk first hdc, hdc in each hdc across; fasten off.

SECOND SHOULDER: With the right side of the Front facing, join 2 strands camel to second marker.

*Row 1:* Ch 2, make 9 (10) hdc across to armhole edge; ch 2, turn. Complete as for other shoulder.

SLEEVES (make 2): Work ribbing as follows: With 2 strands camel and smaller hook, ch 13 (15).

*Row 1:* Sc in second ch from hook and in each ch across—12 (14) sc; ch 1, turn.

*Row 2:* Sc in *back* lp of each sc across; ch 1, turn. Rep Row 2 for 7½ (8) inches. Change to larger hook.

*Foundation row:* Make 30 (32) sc evenly spaced across one long edge; ch 2, turn.

*Row 1* (right side): Sk first sc, hdc in each sc across—30 (32) hdc, counting ch-2 as 1 hdc; ch 2, turn.

*Row 2:* Sk first hdc, hdc in next hdc and in each hdc across, hdc in top of ch-2; ch 2, turn.

Rep last row 2 (0) times.

*Next row:* **Hdc in first hdc—inc made at beg of row;** hdc in each hdc to ch-2, **make 2 hdc in top of ch-2—inc made at end of row**—32 (34) hdc; ch 2, turn.

*Next 5 rows:* Rep Row 2 *and at same time,* inc 1 hdc at each end on next row and every sixth row until there are 40 (42) hdc on row. Work even until total length is 18 (19) inches, ending with wrong-side row; ch 1, turn.

TOP SHAPING: *Row 1:* Sl st in first 3 (4) hdc, ch 2, hdc in next hdc and in each hdc to last 2 (3) hdc, do not work over rem sts—36 hdc; ch 2, turn.

*Row 2:* Dec 1 hdc over next 2 hdc, hdc in each hdc to last 2 hdc, dec 1 hdc over last 2 hdc—34 hdc; ch 2, turn.

*Row 3:* Hdc in next hdc and in each hdc across, hdc in top of ch-2. Rep last 2 rows alternately 4 (5) times—26 (24) hdc.

*Following rows:* Rep Row 2 until 16 sts rem; fasten off.

Sew sleeve seams. Gathering top 16 sts slightly, sew in sleeves, easing to fit.

LOWER RIBBING: Work same as for Sleeve Ribbing until length measures 28 (30) inches; fasten off. Sew narrow edges tog. With ribbing seam at one side of body of sweater, sew ribbing to lower edge, easing to fit.

NECK RIBBING: Beg at narrow edge with 2 strands camel held tog and smaller hook, ch 5. Work as for Sleeve Ribbing over 4 sts until total length measures about 18 (19) inches. Sew narrow edges tog. With seam at center back, sew ribbing to neck opening.

## Knitted Place Mats

Shown on page 42.
Finished size is 13x16 inches.

**MATERIALS**

**For 2 place mats**

Tahki Imports Cotton Creole (100-gram skeins): 5 skeins yellow-gold

Size 9 knitting needles, or size to obtain gauge given below

Cable needle

Size J aluminum crochet hook

**Abbreviations:** Page 217.

**Gauge:** Over pattern stitches, 6 sts = 1 inch.

**INSTRUCTIONS**

Cast on 92 sts. *Row 1:* P 2, * k 4, p 2; rep from * across.

*Row 2 and all even-numbered rows through Row 10:* Knit the k sts and purl the p sts as the work faces you.

*Row 3:* P 2, * sl next 2 sts to cable needle and hold in *back* of work, k 2, k 2 from cable needle, p 2; rep from * across.

*Row 5:* * Sl next 2 sts to cable needle and hold in *back* of work, k 2, p 2 from cable needle, k 2; rep from * across, ending with p 2.

*Row 7:* K 2, * p 2, sl next 2 sts to cable needle and hold in *front* of work, k 2, k 2 from cable needle; rep from * across to last 6 sts, ending with p 2, sl next 2 sts to cable needle and hold in *front* of work, p 2, k 2 from cable needle.

*Row 9:* * Sl 2 sts to cable needle and hold in *front* of work, p 2, k 2 from cable needle, k 2; rep from * across to last 2 sts, ending with p 2. (*Note:* To establish pat rep, work last 2 sts as p 2.)

*Row 10:* Knit the k sts and purl the p sts as the work faces you.

Rep Rows 3–10 seven times more. Bind off, while working Row 3 once more.

EDGING: With crochet hook, work 2 rnds of sc evenly spaced around mat, working (sc, ch 2, sc) in each corner st so work lies flat.

## Crocheted Rug

Shown on page 43.
Finished size is 27x70 inches.

**MATERIALS**

Paternayan Rug Yarn (62-yard skeins): 15 skeins of off-white; 1 skein each of teal, red, spring green, burnt orange, and violet

Sizes 13 and 16 wooden crochet hooks, or sizes to obtain gauge given below

**Abbreviations:** Page 211.

**Gauge:** With smaller hook over sc, 2 sts = 1 inch.

**INSTRUCTIONS**

FIRST COLOR STRIPE: Using smaller hook and teal, ch 60. *Row 1:* Beg in second ch from hook, sc in each ch across—59 sc; ch 1, turn.

*Row 2:* Sc in each sc across to last sc. **Draw up loop in last sc, drop teal, using white, yo and draw through 2 lps on hook—color change made;** ch 1, turn. Fasten off teal.

FIRST PATTERN BAND: *Row 1:* Sc in each sc across; ch 1, turn.

*Row 2:* Sc in *front* lp of first st, * sc in *both* lps of next st, sc in *front* lp of next st; rep from * across, ch 1, turn.

*Row 3:* Sc in *both* lps of first st, * sc in *back* lp of next st, sc in *both* lps of next st; rep from * across, ch 1, turn.

Rep Rows 2–3 alternately until length of pat band measures 4 inches, changing to red at end of last row. Fasten off off-white.

*Note:* So each color stripe looks consistent, always begin a color stripe at the right-hand edge. If the pat band measures 4 inches at the end of a right-side row, fasten off and begin the color stripe at the right-hand edge.

SECOND COLOR STRIPE: With red, sc evenly for 2 rows, changing to off-white at end of second row; ch 1, turn.

SECOND PATTERN BAND: *Row 1:* Sc in first sc, * **draw up lp in next st, ch 3 (working chs through first lp on hook only), yo and draw through both lps on hook—bobble made;** sc in next st; rep from * across; ch 1, turn.

*Row 2:* Sc in each st across; ch 1, turn.

*Row 3:* Sc in first st, * sc in next st, bobble in next st; rep from * across, ending with sc in last st; ch 1, turn. *Row 4:* Rep Row 2.

Rep Rows 1–4 until total length of pat band is 4 inches, changing to green at end of last row; ch 1, turn. Fasten off off-white.

THIRD COLOR STRIPE: *Row 1:* With green, sc in each sc across; ch 1, turn.

*Row 2:* **Draw up lp in each of next 2 sc, yo, draw through 3 lps on hook—dec made.** Sc in each sc to last 2 sc, work dec over next 2 sc, changing to off-white to complete the dec—57 sts; ch 1, turn.

THIRD PATTERN BAND: *Row 1:* In first sc work **sc, ch 1, sc—V-st made.** * Sk 1 sc, V-st in next sc; rep from * across; ch 1, turn.

*Row 2:* * V-st in ch-1 sp of next V-st, ch 1; rep from * across; ch 1, turn.

Rep Row 2 until length of pat band is 4 inches, changing to burnt orange at end of last row; ch 1, turn. Fasten off off-white.

FOURTH COLOR STRIPE: *Row 1:* With burnt orange, work sc in each sc across row (sk ch-1 sts), and inc 1 st at *each* end of row; ch 1, turn.

*Row 2:* Sc in each sc across, changing to off-white at end of row—59 sts; ch 1, turn.

FOURTH PATTERN BAND: *Row 1:* In first sc work **sc, hdc—cluster (cl) made.** * Sk sc, cl in next st. Rep from * across, ending with cl in last st; ch 1, turn.

*Row 2:* Cl in sc of last cl made in Row 1, * cl in sc of next cl in previous row; rep from * across, ending with cl in last st; ch 1, turn.

Rep Row 2 until length of pat band measures 4 inches, changing to violet at end of last row; ch 1, turn. Fasten off off-white.

FIFTH COLOR STRIPE: With violet, sc in each st for 2 rows; inc 4 sts evenly spaced on second row and change to off-white at end of second row—63 sts. Ch 1, turn. Fasten off violet.

FIFTH PATTERN BAND: *Row 1:* With larger hook, sk first sc, * sc in next sc, sc in space following the skipped st (and around sc just made), sk next sc; rep from * across, ending with sc in last st. Ch 1, turn.

Rep Row 1 until length of pat band measures 4 inches, changing to teal at end of last row; ch 1, turn. Fasten off white. Change to smaller hook.

SIXTH COLOR STRIPE: Using teal, sc in each st for 2 rows and dec 4 sts evenly spaced across the first row—59 sts.

Rep from First Pat Band and work until 15 color stripes and 15 pat bands have been worked. Work 2 rows of sc with teal. Fasten off. Weave in yarn ends; block.

# INSPIRATIONS FROM YOUR CHILDREN'S PAINTINGS

***Kids' artwork provides a homegrown source of design ideas that's hard to beat for impact and originality. In this chapter you'll discover ways to translate your young Picasso's best efforts into unusual knit and crochet projects that the entire family can enjoy.***

Here's a crayon-bright pullover that's truly a "young designer" original. Copied directly from a child's painting of a friend and her dog, the figures and landscape details are first transferred to graph paper and then sized to fit the front of a classic crewneck sweater.

When working with original drawings, you can knit in the motifs as you stitch the sweater, or work them in duplicate stitch after the knitting is complete. Use the pattern provided for the design shown here, or adapt one of your child's own favorite drawings to suit the front of any pullover. Directions begin on page 198.

# Inspirations From Your Children's Paintings

A child's-eye view of a sailboat provides the common motif for this seaworthy pair of sweaters.

Escorted by seagulls, one boat sets sail front and center on the long-sleeved pullover, *far right*. "Port" and "starboard" sleeves knitted in different colors add an authentically nautical note. (Work these or any whimsical words on the sleeves of your own child's sweater using duplicate-stitch embroidery.) On the short-sleeve version, *near right,* a trio of smaller ships races across the bottom half of the sweater. See page 199 for instructions.

# INSPIRATIONS FROM YOUR CHILDREN'S PAINTINGS

To continue the nautical theme, stitch a flotilla of sailing ships across each end of a colorful crocheted throw. Worked in afghan stitch, the design pictured here measures 41x52 inches.

You can use almost any drawing in a project like this. Just chart the motif on a grid. Next, count the number of squares in the design to determine how many stitches and rows you need to crochet to make the background for a single motif. Next, add a few stitches between motifs (we added five between each boat), determine the number of motifs you wish to include, and calculate the stitch width of the afghan you wish to make. After stitching the afghan, cross-stitch the motifs in place, as shown *below.*

For more complete instructions, see page 200.

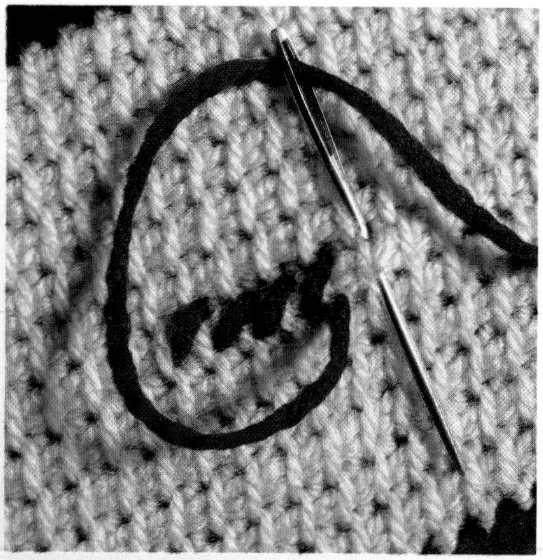

*Knitting and Crocheting the Classics*

# SWEATERS AND AFGHANS

***Time-honored craft favorites—ribs and cables, granny squares, Arans, even argyles, Fair Isles, and ripples—are combined in this collection of best-loved stitches and patterns.***

***Whether you find an old favorite or begin a new challenge, expect these treasured patterns to become your own classics.***

Your family will look shipshape decked out in these quick-to-knit cardigans. Classic styling, with notched collars, roomy patch pockets, and wooden toggle buttons, makes them everyone's favorites. The wide-rib pattern works up easily, using double strands of yarn and Size 11 needles, and simple armhole and shoulder shapings make them ideal projects for beginners. For directions, see page 70.

# SWEATERS AND AFGHANS

Few men can resist a sweater knit just for them, especially when it's as comfortably styled as the crewneck pullover, *right.* Classic cables and neutral tones are sure to make this sweater a favorite. The crewneck features dropped shoulders and a roomy ribbed neckline. Its generous cut ensures an easy fit over fall's heftier fabrics. And the tweedy texture complements the season's richly colored clothes.

If you have admired the intricate knitting of Scandinavian ski sweaters, the pair of richly patterned afghans, *opposite,* will warm your heart. They are knitted in the same two-color technique and feature adaptations of classic geometric patterns and snowflake motifs.

The houndstooth afghan sports oversize designs and wide snowflake panel borders. The Nordic sampler is striped with four different designs in traditional ski sweater colors. Both are worked in one piece from end to end and measure approximately 46x60 inches when completed.

The rich hues of autumn color these afghans, but other color combinations could be just as attractive. You may wish to consider an array of subtle pastel shades or even a trio of bright primaries.

# SWEATERS AND AFGHANS

Traditionally stitched into sturdy sweaters by the fishing folk of the British Isles, fisherman-style knitting is distinguished by its exquisite patterning and exemplary crafting. The beautiful raised-pattern stitches create a distinctive style of knitting that has inspired generations of knitters to show off their crafting skills.

Rough and ready-to-go sweaters like the fisherman knits, *above,* are just the thing for energetic youngsters. This sporty pair of hooded sweaters displays a handsome variety of textured stitches including cables, popcorns, and double-seed stitch. Her jacket sports a zippered front closure and two knitted-in pockets. His pullover, styled like a hooded sweatshirt, comes complete with a pocket pouch. Both are knitted with a washable worsted-weight yarn.

The fisherman-look afghan, *opposite,* is worked in four fun-to-knit cabled and patterned panels. Each identical panel is stitched individually, then crocheted together to create the multitextured effect. When complete, this generously proportioned afghan measures 72x73 inches and is large enough to wrap up in by the fire or to cover a guest bed on a chilly night.

TOURI
JEWELRY
CHAS. W

# SWEATERS AND AFGHANS

Striking colors and clever techniques turn the most traditional designs into stitchery standouts.

This blue and black afghan is an oversize version of a traditional ripple pattern. You can knit it with 100 percent wool yarn in the creative color combination shown here, or choose colors that complement your own decor. When completed, this cozy throw measures 54x70 inches.

Most crocheters learn how to make a basic granny square before anything else. The pair of pullovers here have granny square fronts that are worked with two strands of yarn held together—a small amount of colored yarn and a strand of off-white—to create a tweedy look. The backs, sleeves, and yokes are worked in rows of half-double crochet stitches.

The adult sizes are worked with knitting worsted; the child sizes are stitched with sport yarn.

# SWEATERS AND AFGHANS

Traditional patterns always are favorites no matter what the season. These classic sweaters in Fair Isle and argyle patterns boast contemporary colors that will complement the rich earth tones of fall and winter as well as the pastel palettes of spring and summer fashions.

The woman's V-neck Fair Isle vest is worked in stockinette stitch (knit one row, purl one row), using sport yarn in subtle shades of pinks, roses, and tans against a striking slate background. (See the detail photograph, *below*.) Six different geometric and snowflake patterns stripe both the front and back of this classic vest.

The classic styling and oversize argyle design of the man's cardigan make this the perfect project for beginners who are eager to try their hand at two-color knitting. Soft mauves and shades of a grayed purple accent the argyle pattern that appears on the front of this cardigan.

If the man in your life prefers more neutral tones, you may wish to knit this sweater in tan, with brown and cream accents. The entire sweater is knitted with worsted-weight yarn in stockinette stitch, with duplicate-stitch embroidery creating the crossbars on the argyles.

# SWEATERS AND AFGHANS

Some of the very best sweater designs have simple lines that never seem to go out of fashion. Indeed, simple styling makes a great project for beginners who want quick results with a fashionable difference. Accomplished knitters, too, will appreciate the ease of crafting an uncomplicated sweater, especially when the end result is good looks and style.

The timeless pair of pullovers pictured here are classically styled with high-quality yarns—a practical combination that ensures a sweater's design will have lasting quality and enduring appeal.

Even novice knitters can master the basket weave stitch that patterns this pair of sporty pullovers. It's simply a variation of basic knit and purl stitches. Just as easy to knit are the rows of garter stitch that accent the waist, wrists, and neckline of each sweater.

These classic crewnecks are worked with a softly flecked wool yarn that creates a look that is textured and subtly tweeded—a perfect complement to cool-weather casuals. With only a few changes, you can knit this sweater for any season. Simply substitute a cotton yarn of equal weight and you will have a snappy sweater that is sure to add zest and spirit to any number of spring and summer separates.

## Child's Cardigan

Shown on pages 58–59.
Directions are for Size Small (4–6); changes for Medium (8–10) and Large (12–14) follow in parentheses. Chest measurements = 21¾ (26¾, 31¾) inches.

**MATERIALS**

Lion Brand 100 percent wool knitting worsted yarn *or* Lion Brand "Pamela" acrylic worsted-weight yarn (4-ounce skeins): 7 (7, 7) skeins of No. 109 Colonial Blue

Sizes 9 and 10 knitting needles, or sizes to obtain gauge below

Size H aluminum crochet hook

Six toggle buttons

**Abbreviations:** Pages 211 and 217.
**Gauge:** With larger needles over pat st, 4 sts = 1 inch using 2 strands of yarn.

**INSTRUCTIONS**

*Note:* Cardigan is worked with double strands of yarn throughout.

PATTERN STITCH: ***Row 1:* K 3, * p 2, k 3; rep from * across. *Row 2:* P 3, * k 2, p 3; rep from * across.** These 2 rows make up pat.

BACK: With two strands of yarn and larger needles, cast on 43 (53, 63) sts. Work even in pat until total length from beg measures 9 (11½, 12½) inches, or desired length to underarm.

ARMHOLE SHAPING: Bind off 3 (3, 4) sts at beg of next 2 rows. Dec 1 st at each end every other row 1 (1, 3) time—35 (45, 49) sts. Work even in pat until total length past beg of armhole measures 4½ (6½, 7) inches.

SHOULDER SHAPING: Bind off 6 (8, 8) sts at beg of next 2 rows. Bind off 5 (7, 8) sts at beg of next 2 rows. Bind off rem 13 (15, 17) sts for Back neck.

LEFT FRONT: With two strands of yarn and larger needles, cast on 22 (27, 32) sts. *Row 1:* * K 3, p 2. Rep from * to last 7 sts; ending k 1, (p 1, k 1) 3 times.

*Row 2:* (P 1, k 1) 3 times; p 1, * k 2, p 3. Rep from * to end. These 2 rows make up pat. Work even in pat as established until total length measures same as Back to underarm, ending with Row 2.

ARMHOLE SHAPING: Bind off 3 (3, 4) sts at beg of next row; work 1 row even. *Next row:* Dec 1 st at armhole edge every other row 1 (1, 3) time—18 (23, 25) sts. Work even until total length past beg of armhole measures 2½ (4, 4½) inches, ending at front edge.

NECK SHAPING: Bind off 5 (6, 7) sts at beg of next row; work one row even. Dec 1 st at neck edge every other row 2 times—11 (15, 16) sts. Work even until total length past beg of armhole measures 4½ (6½, 7) inches, ending at armhole edge.

SHOULDER SHAPING: Bind off 6 (8, 8) sts; complete row. *Next row:* Work even. Bind off rem 5 (7, 8) sts; complete row.

RIGHT FRONT: Work as for Left Front, reversing pats and shapings.

SLEEVES: With two strands of yarn and larger needles, cast on 23 (23, 28) sts. Work even in pat for 2½ (3½, 3½) inches. Inc 1 st each end every 2 (1, 1¼) inches 4 (10, 9) times—31 (43, 46) sts. Work even until length measures 11 (14, 16) inches, or desired length to underarm, ending with Row 2 of pat. *Note:* Sleeve length allows for a turned cuff of 1½ (2, 2) inches.

ARMHOLE SHAPING: Bind off 3 (3, 4) sts at beg of next 2 rows. Dec 1 st at each end every other row 9 (11, 13) times. *Sizes Medium and Large only:* Bind off 3 sts at beg of next 2 rows. Bind off rem 7 (9, 6) sts.

POCKET (make 2): With two strands of yarn and larger needles, cast on 13 (18, 18) sts. Work even in pat until total length measures 2¼ (3½, 3½) inches. Work in k 1, p 1 ribbing for 1 inch; bind off *loosely* in ribbing.

COLLAR: With two strands of yarn and smaller needles, cast on 19 (21, 25) sts. * K 1, p 1; rep from * across. Cast on 6 (8, 9) sts at beg of next 4 rows—43 (53, 61) sts. Work in k 1, p 1 ribbing until length past last inc row measures 4 (4, 4) inches. Bind off *loosely* in ribbing.

TOGGLE LOOPS (make 3): With single yarn and crochet hook, ch 32. Sl st in second ch from hook and in each ch across. Fasten off, leaving an end for sewing. Join ch to form circle. With joining at center, tack tog at center to form a figure eight.

FINISHING: Sew side and shoulder seams. Set in sleeves. With center back of collar at center back of neck, sew collar in place, leaving 4 (4, 4) sts free at each front edge.

Sew on pockets even with bottom edges. Sew buttons on the 2 p sts at inside edge of k 1, p 1 Right Front band. Position the uppermost pair of buttons flush to neck edge, and lowest pair at waist. Space remaining pair evenly bet. Sew on toggle loops.

# Woman's Cardigan

Shown on pages 58–59.
Directions are for Size Small (12); changes for Medium (14) and Large (16) follow in parentheses. Bust measurements = 34 (36½, 37¾) inches.

**MATERIALS**
Lion Brand 100 percent wool knitting worsted yarn *or* Lion Brand "Pamela" acrylic worsted-weight yarn (4-ounce skeins): 8 (8, 8) skeins No. 109 Colonial Blue
Sizes 9 and 10 knitting needles, or sizes to obtain gauge given below
Size H aluminum crochet hook
Six toggle buttons

**Abbreviations:** Pages 211 and 217.
**Gauge:** With larger needles over pat st, 4 sts = 1 inch using 2 strands of yarn.

**INSTRUCTIONS**
*Note:* Cardigan is worked with double strands of yarn throughout.

PATTERN STITCH: ***Row 1:* K 3, * p 2, k 3; rep from * across. *Row 2:* P 3, * k 2, p 3; rep from * across.** These 2 rows make up pat.

BACK: With two strands of yarn and larger needles, cast on 68 (68, 73) sts. Work even in pat until total length from beg measures 17 (17, 17) inches, or desired length to the underarm.

ARMHOLE SHAPING: Bind off 4 (4, 4) sts at beg of next 2 rows. Dec 1 st at each end every other row 3 (2, 3) times—54 (56, 59) sts. Work even in pat until total length past beg of armhole measures 7½ (7¾, 8) inches.

SHOULDER SHAPING: Bind off 6 (6, 7) sts at beg of next 2 rows. Bind off 6 (6, 6) sts at beg of next 4 rows. Bind off rem 18 (20, 21) sts for Back neck.

LEFT FRONT: With two strands of yarn and larger needles, cast on 34 (39, 39) sts. *Row 1:* * K 3, p 2; rep from * to last 9 sts; ending k 1, (p 1, k 1) 4 times.

*Row 2:* (P 1, k 1) 4 times; p 1, * k 2, p 3; rep from * to end. These 2 rows make up pat. Work even in pat as established until total length measures same as Back to underarm, ending with Row 2.

ARMHOLE SHAPING: Bind off 4 (4, 4) sts at beg of next row; work 1 row even. Dec 1 st at armhole edge every other row 3 (2, 3) times—27 (33, 32) sts. Work even until total length past beg of armhole shaping measures 4½ (4¾, 5) inches, ending at front edge.

NECK SHAPING: Bind off 7 (10, 10) sts at beg of next row; complete row. Work one row even. Dec 1 st at neck edge every other row 2 (5, 3) times—18 (18, 19) sts. Work even until total length past beg of armhole measures 7½ (7¾, 8) inches, ending at armhole edge.

SHOULDER SHAPING: Bind off 6 (6, 7) sts at beg of row; complete row. Work 1 row even. Bind off 6 (6, 6) sts; complete row. Work 1 row even. Bind off rem 6 (6, 6) sts.

RIGHT FRONT: Work as for Left Front, reversing pats and shapings.

SLEEVES: With two strands of yarn and larger needles, cast on 33 (33, 33) sts. Work even in pat for 3½ inches. Inc 1 st at each end every 1½ inches 8 (9, 9) times—49 (51, 51) sts. Work even until total length measures 19¼ (19½, 19¾) inches or desired length to underarm, ending with Row 2 of pat. (*Note:* Sleeve length allows for a turned back cuff of 2 inches.)

ARMHOLE SHAPING: Bind off 4 (4, 4) sts at beg of next 2 rows. Dec 1 st at each end every other row 15 times. Bind off rem 11 (13, 13) sts.

POCKET (make 2): With two strands of yarn and larger needles, cast on 18 (18, 18) sts. Work even in pat until total length measures 3½ (3½, 3½) inches. Work in k 1, p 1 ribbing for 1 inch; bind off *loosely* in ribbing.

COLLAR: With two strands of yarn and smaller needles, cast on 25 (27, 29) sts. Work in k 1, p 1 ribbing across row. Cast on 9 (11, 11) sts at beg of next 4 rows—61 (71, 73) sts. Work in ribbing as established until length past last inc row measures 4½ inches. Bind off *loosely* in ribbing.

TOGGLE LOOPS (make 3): With single strand of yarn and crochet hook, ch 36. Sl st in second ch from hook and in each ch across. Fasten off, leaving an end for sewing. Join ch to form circle. With joining at center, tack tog at center to form a figure eight.

FINISHING: Sew side, shoulder, and sleeve seams. Set in sleeves. With center back of collar at center back of neck, sew collar in place, leaving 6 (6, 6) sts free at front edges.

Sew on pockets even with bottom edges. Sew buttons on the 2 p sts, leaving the k 1, p 1 sts free. Position the uppermost pair of buttons flush to neck edge; lowest pair at waist, centering middle pair bet. Sew on toggle loops.

*continued*

## Man's Cardigan

Shown on pages 58–59.
Instructions are for Size Small (40); changes for Medium (44) and Large (46) follow in parentheses. Chest sizes = 40 (44, 46) inches.

**MATERIALS**

Lion Brand 100 percent wool knitting worsted yarn *or* Lion Brand "Pamela" acrylic worsted-weight yarn (4-ounce skeins): 8 (8, 8) skeins of No. 109 Colonial Blue
Sizes 9 and 10 knitting needles, or sizes to obtain gauge given below
Size H aluminum crochet hook
Eight toggle buttons

**Abbreviations:** Pages 211 and 217.
**Gauge:** With larger needles over pat st, 4 sts = 1 inch using 2 strands of yarn.

**INSTRUCTIONS**

*Note:* Cardigan is worked with double strands of yarn throughout.

PATTERN STITCH: ***Row 1:* K 3, * p 2, k 3; rep from * across. *Row 2:* P 3, * k 2, p 3; rep from * across.** These 2 rows make up pat.

BACK: With two strands of yarn and larger needles, cast on 78 (83, 93) sts. Work even in pat until total length from beg measures 19 inches, or desired length to underarm.

ARMHOLE SHAPING: Bind off 4 (4, 4) sts at beg of next 2 rows. Dec 1 st at each end every other row 1 (2, 6) time—68 (71, 73) sts. Work even in pat until total length past beg of armhole measures 9 (10, 10½) inches.

SHOULDER SHAPING: Bind off 8 sts at beg of next 2 rows; bind off 7 (8, 8) sts at beg of next 2 rows; bind off 7 (7, 8) sts at beg of next 2 rows. Bind off rem 24 (25, 25) sts for back of neck.

LEFT FRONT: With two strands of yarn and larger needles, cast on 41 (46, 46) sts. *Row 1:* * K 3, p 2; rep from * to last 11 sts; ending k 1, (p 1, k 1) 5 times.

*Row 2:* (P 1, k 1) 5 times; p 1, * k 2, p 3; rep from * across. These 2 rows make up pat. Work even in pat as established until total length measures same as Back to underarm, ending with Row 2.

ARMHOLE SHAPING: Bind off 4 (4, 4) sts at beg of next row; complete row. Work 1 row even. Dec 1 st at armhole edge every other row 1 (2, 6) time—36 (40, 36) sts. Work even until total length past beg of armhole measures 5 (6, 6½) inches, ending at front edge.

NECK SHAPING: Bind off 11 (12, 10) sts at beg of next row; complete row. Work 1 row even. Dec 1 st at neck edge every other row 3 (5, 2) times—22 (23, 24) sts. Work even until total length past beg of armhole measures 9 (10, 10½) inches, ending at armhole edge.

SHOULDER SHAPING: Bind off 8 (8, 8) sts; complete row. Work 1 row even. Bind off 7 (8, 8) sts at beg of next row; complete row. Work one row even. Bind off rem 7 (7, 8) sts.

RIGHT FRONT: Work as for Left Front, reversing pats and shapings.

SLEEVES: With two strands of yarn and larger needles, cast on 38 (38, 38) sts. Work in pat for 4 inches. Inc 1 st at each end every 1¼ (1, 1) inches 11 (14, 15) times—60 (66, 68) sts. Work even until total length measures 21 (22, 22½) inches or desired length to underarm, ending with Row 2 of pat. (*Note:* Sleeve length allows for turned cuff of 2½ inches.)

ARMHOLE SHAPING: Bind off 4 (4, 4) sts at beg of next 2 rows. Dec 1 st at each end every other row 17 (14, 13) times. Dec 1 st each end every row 3 (9, 11) times. Bind off rem 12 (12, 12) sts.

POCKET (make 2): With two strands of yarn and larger needles, cast on 18 sts. Work even in pat until total length measures 3½ inches. Work in k 1, p 1 ribbing for 1 inch; bind off *loosely* in ribbing.

COLLAR: With two strands of yarn and smaller needles, cast on 35 (35, 35) sts. Work in k 1, p 1 ribbing across row. Cast on 12 (12, 14) sts at beg of next 4 rows—83 (83, 91) sts. Work in ribbing as established until length past last inc row measures 5 inches. Bind off *loosely* in ribbing.

TOGGLE LOOPS (make 4): With single strand of yarn and crochet hook, ch 38. Sl st in second ch from hook and in each ch across. Fasten off, leaving an end for sewing. Join ch to form circle. With joining at center, tack tog at center to form a figure eight.

FINISHING: Sew side, shoulder, and sleeve seams. Set in sleeves. With center back of collar at center back of neck, sew collar in place, leaving 6 sts free at each front edge.

Sew on pockets even with bottom edges. Sew buttons on the p sts, leaving the k 1, p 1 sts free. Position the uppermost pair of buttons flush to neck edge; place lowest pair at waist, and space remaining two pairs evenly bet. Sew on toggle

# Nordic Afghan

Shown on page 61.
Finished size is 46x60 inches.

**MATERIALS**

Worsted-weight yarn (3½-ounce skeins): 6 skeins of blue, 5 skeins each of cream and rust, 2 skeins of gray
1 skein (50 grams) of blue sport or sock yarn
36-inch-long Size 10½ circular knitting needle
Size 2 straight knitting needles
Size H aluminum crochet hook
Tapestry needle

**Abbreviations:** Page 217.
**Gauge:** With larger needles, 9 sts = 2 inches.

**INSTRUCTIONS**

**For the afghan**

With gray and circular needle, cast on 155 sts. Work 4 rows in garter st (k every row). Cast on 3 sts at end of last row and join, taking care not to twist work. Afghan now begins to work in rounds. Knit all rnds unless stated otherwise and *always* purl the 3 cast-on stitches.

Work from charts, *right,* to establish pats. Work 9 rnds of Chart 1; rep from A to B around, working last 5 sts before cast-on sts from B to C.

Work Chart 2; rep from A to B around, work last st before cast-on sts at C.

Work Chart 4; rep from A to B around, work last st before cast-on sts at C.

Rep Chart 2 as cited above.

Rep Chart 1 reversing order of rows working from D to A. Work 1 rnd cream, 2 rnds gray, p 1 rnd gray, k 1 rnd gray, p 1 rnd gray, k 1 rnd gray. Break off cream and gray.

Attach blue and rust. Work 26 rnds of Chart 3 (chart shows 10 rows only); rep from A to B around, work last 5 sts before cast-on sts from B to C. Work rows from A to D twice, then work from A to E to complete pattern.

K 1 rnd cream and rep Chart 1.

Work 11 rnds of Chart 3.

Work Chart 2. Work 11 rnds of Chart 3. Work Chart 1 from D to A. Work 26 rnds of Chart 3.

P 1 rnd in gray, k 1 rnd in gray, p 1 rnd in gray, k 2 rnds in gray, k 1 rnd in cream.

Work Chart 1 from A to D. Work 1 rnd cream; rep Chart 2; then rep Chart 4; rep Chart 2; rep Chart 1 from D to A. Break off all colors except gray.

K 1 rnd gray. Bind off 3 cast-on sts and work 4 garter st rows in gray. Bind off.

With sewing machine set for overcast or zigzag stitch, *and working through one thickness only of afghan,* sew length of p ridge as closely as possible to first k st on body of afghan. At end, turn work and stitch along same side of ridge. Rep steps on the other side of p ridge. Set afghan aside.

**For the facings**

Make two. With smaller needles and sport or sock yarn, cast on 10 sts. Work even in st st (k 1 row, p 1 row) until total length equals that of afghan. Bind off. Steam both facings flat.

**To assemble**

Lay afghan out with the right side up. Line up one facing on top of p ridge with left edge covering right-hand edge of afghan sts; whipstitch facings in place.

Turn afghan around so facing just sewn to afghan is on right. Rep process with second facing. Fold and pin facings back to expose p ridge. Cut afghan open between rows of machine stitching. Turn afghan wrong side up and fold facings to wrong side and stitch down free edge of facing, covering machine stitching and loose ends. Block to complete.

**For the fringe**

Cut 155 ten-inch lengths from both rust and blue worsted-weight yarn. Alternating colors, fold a length in half; knot in cast-on and bind-off sts using crochet hook.

**NORDIC AFGHAN**

**Chart 4**

**Chart 3**

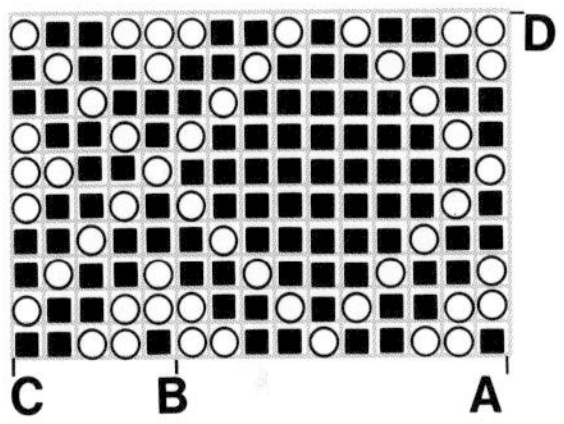


**Chart 2**

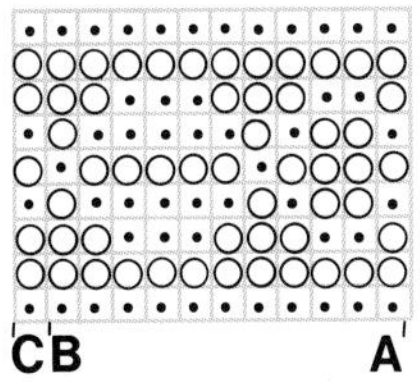


**Color Key**

⊡ Cream
☒ Grey
▣ Blue
◘ Rust

**Chart 1**

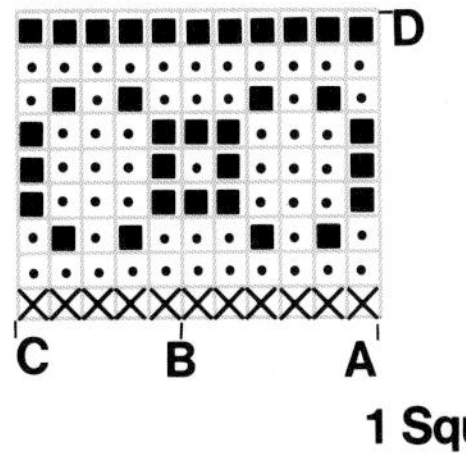


**1 Square = 1 Stitch**

# Houndstooth Afghan

Shown on page 61.
Finished size is 48x60 inches.

**MATERIALS**

Bulky yarn in the following amounts and colors (100-gram balls): 13 balls of cream, 6 balls of rust, and 11 balls of brown, *or* substitute two strands (worked together) of worsted-weight yarn in the colors of your choice and adjust amounts accordingly
1 ball (100 grams) of dark brown sport yarn for facings
36-inch-long Size 11 circular knitting needles, or size to obtain gauge given below
Size 1 straight knitting needles
Size I aluminum crochet hook

**Abbreviations:** Page 217.
**Gauge:** With Size 11 needles, 5 sts = 2 inches.

**INSTRUCTIONS**

**For the afghan**

With Size 11 needles and cream, cast on 119 sts. Knit 2 rows with cream. Cast on 4 sts; join, taking care not to twist sts. (*Note:* Work now begins to work in rounds. Knit all sts except the 4 cast-on sts; always purl the cast-on sts.)

Following Chart No. 1, *right,* work around, beginning at A and ending at B for pat repeat. Work last 11 sts (before the cast-on sts) from A to C. Work 19 rnds of Chart 1 pat until 5 pats of brown checks are completed.

Break off brown. Join rust and k 3 rnds; k one rnd cream.

Work 27 rnds of Chart No. 2. Work from A to B 4 times, from B to D once, and from C to D 3 times. Work one rnd cream and 2 rnds rust. Break off rust; attach brown.

Work Chart No. 1 until 18 brown checks have been completed. Break off brown. Join rust. K 2 rnds in rust, then one rnd in cream. Work 27 rnds of Chart No. 2. Work 1 rnd cream, 3 rnds rust. Break off rust.

Attach brown and work Chart No. 1 for 19 rnds until 5 brown checks have been completed. Bind off 4 p sts at end of last rnd. Knit 2 rows in cream. Bind off.

**For the facings**

Make 2. With sport yarn and Size 1 needles, cast on 8 sts. Work even in st st (k 1 row, p 1 row) until total length of facing equals that of afghan. Steam both facings flat.

**To assemble**

Complete as for Nordic afghan, page 73.

**For the fringe**

Cut 242 twelve-inch lengths of brown yarn. Fold each length in half and using a crochet hook, knot folded lengths individually in each cast-on and bind-off st across ends of afghan.

**HOUNDSTOOTH AFGHAN**

**Chart 2**

D C B A

**Chart 1**

D

B C A

**Color Key**

× Brown
◣ Cream
○ Rust

**1 Square = 1 Stitch**

# Man's Cabled Pullover

Shown on page 60.
Directions are for Size 38; changes for Sizes 40 and 42 follow in parentheses. Chest = 40 (42, 44) inches when slightly stretched.

**MATERIALS**
Phildar Palmares (50-gram skeins): 16 (18, 18) skeins of No. 23 brown/taupe
Sizes 6 and 8 knitting needles, or size to obtain gauge given below
Size 6 double-pointed needles
Cable needle; stitch holder

**Abbreviations:** Page 217.
**Gauge:** With larger needles and 2 strands yarn held tog over pat st, 15 sts = 4 inches; 23 rows = 4 inches.

**INSTRUCTIONS**
BACK: With smaller needles and 2 strands yarn held tog, cast on 78 (82, 86) sts. Work k 1, p 1 ribbing for 3½ inches, inc 6 sts evenly spaced on last row—84 (88, 92) sts. Change to larger needles and beg pat st as follows:

*Rows 1, 3, 5, 9, 13, 17, 21, 23, and 25:* P 6 (8, 10), * k 6, p 5; rep from * 6 times more, ending with p 1 (3, 5).

*Row 2 and every even-numbered row through Row 26:* K the k sts and p the p sts as the work faces you.

*Rows 7 and 15:* P 6 (8, 10), * k 2, sl next 2 sts to cable needle and hold in *back* of work, k 2, k 2 from cable needle, p 5; rep from * 6 times more, ending with p 1 (3, 5).

*Rows 11 and 19:* P 6 (8, 10), * sl next 2 sts to cable needle and hold in *front* of work, k 2, k 2 from cable needle, k 2, p 5; rep from * 6 times more, ending with p 1 (3, 5). Rep Rows 1–26 for pat.

Work even until total length measures 17¾ inches. Mark each end of last row for underarm. Work even until total length measures 27¼ (27½, 28) inches.

NECK SHAPING: Work across row in pat and *at same time* bind off center 30 (30, 32) sts for neck edge. Attach a second ball of yarn and work each side separately. Work even for 2 rows. Bind off rem 27 (29, 30) sts for each shoulder.

FRONT: Work same as for Back until total length measures 24¼ (24½, 24¾) inches.

FRONT NECK SHAPING: Work across row in pat and *at same time* bind off center 10 (10, 10) sts for neck edge. Attach a second ball of yarn and work each side separately, binding off at neck edge only on every other row as follows: 3 (3, 4) sts once, 2 (2, 3) sts once, 2 (2, 2) sts once, then 1 st 3 (3, 2) times.

When total length to shoulder equals that of Back, bind off rem 27 (29, 30) sts.

SLEEVES: With smaller needles and 2 strands yarn held tog, cast on 36 (38, 40) sts. Work k 1, p 1 ribbing for 3 inches, inc 8 (10, 10) sts evenly spaced on last row—44 (48, 50) sts. Change to larger needles and establish Row 1 of cable pat as follows: P 8 (10, 11), * k 6, p 5; rep from * twice, end p 3 (5, 6). Continue to work 3 cables as for Back and *at the same time* inc 1 st at beg and end of every fourth row 3 (3, 4) times, then every sixth row 13 (13, 12) times, keeping inc sts in reverse st st (p right-side rows, k wrong-side rows)—76 (80, 82) sts. Work even until total length measures 19½ (19½, 19) inches. Bind off loosely. Sew shoulder seams.

NECKBAND: With double-pointed needles and 2 strands of yarn held tog, pick up and k 74 (74, 78) sts evenly spaced around neckline. Work k 1, p 1 ribbing for 2¼ inches. Bind off loosely in ribbing.

FINISHING: Sew sleeves to shoulders bet markers. Sew the side and sleeve seams. Fold the neckband to the wrong side; tack in place.

# Fisherman Knit Afghan

Shown on page 63.
Finished size is 72x73 inches.

**MATERIALS**
Acrylic 4-ply worsted-weight yarn (3½-ounce skeins): 23 skeins
Size 7 knitting needles, or size to obtain gauge given below
1 cable or double-pointed needle
Size H crochet hook
6 markers

**Abbreviations:** Page 217.
**Gauge:** Over st st, 5 sts = 1 inch.

**INSTRUCTIONS**
*Note:* Afghan is made of 4 identical panels that are knitted separately and crocheted together.

**For one panel**
Cast on 82 sts. *Row 1:* (K 2, p 2) twice; k 2, place marker. P 5, k 4, p 5, place marker. P 10, place marker. P 2, k 10, p 2, place marker. P 10, place marker. P 5, k 4, p 5, place marker. (K 2, p 2) twice; k 2.

*Note:* Always slip markers.

*Row 2:* (P 2, k 2) twice; p 2, k 5, p 4, k 17, p 10, k 17, p 4, k 5, (p 2, k 2) twice; p 2.

*Row 3:* (P 2, k 2) twice; p 2, [p 4, sl 1 st to cable needle and hold in *back* of work, k 2, k into *back* lp of st on cable needle, sl 2 sts to cable needle and hold in *front* of work, p 1, k 2 sts from cable needle, p 4]; p 12, k 10, p 12. Rep bet [ ]s once. (P 2, k 2) twice; p 2.

*Note:* Sts between first and second markers and between fifth and sixth markers form diamond pat with twisted rib in center of diamond. All k sts in the center of the diamond are knit in the back lp, written "k 1-b."

*Row 4:* (K 2, p 2) twice; k 2, [k 4, p 2, k 1-b, p 3, k 4], k 12, p 10, k 12. Rep bet [ ]s. (K 2, p 2) twice; k 2.

*continued*

*Row 5:* (K 2, p 2) twice; k 2, [p 3, sl 1 to cable needle and hold in *back* of work, k 2, p 1 from cable needle, k 1-b, p 1, sl 2 to cable needle and hold in *front* of work, k 1-b, k 2 from cable needle, p 3], p 12, k 10, p 12. Rep bet [ ]s. (K 2, p 2) twice; k 2.

*Row 6:* (P 2, k 2) twice; p 2, [k 3, p 3, k 1-b, p 1, k 1-b, p 2, k 3], k 12, p 10, k 12. Rep bet [ ]s. (P 2, k 2) twice; p 2.

*Row 7:* (P 2, k 2) twice; p 2, [p 2, sl 1 to cable needle and hold in *back* of work, k 2, k 1-b from cable needle, (p 1, k 1-b) twice; sl 2 to cable needle and hold in *front* of work, p 1, k 2 from cable needle, p 2], p 12, k 10, p 12. Rep bet [ ]s. (P 2, k 2) twice; p 2.

*Row 8:* (K 2, p 2) twice; k 2, [k 2, p 2, (k 1-b, p 1) 3 times; p 2, k 2], k 12, p 10, k 12. Rep bet [ ]s. (K 2, p 2) twice; k 2.

*Row 9:* (K 2, p 2) twice; k 2, [p 1, sl 1 to cable needle and hold in *back* of work, k 2, p 1 from cable needle, (k 1-b, p 1) 3 times; sl 2 to cable needle and hold in *front* of work, k 1-b, k 2 from cable needle, p 1], p 12, k 10, p 12, rep bet [ ]s. (K 2, p 2) twice; k 2.

*Row 10:* (P 2, k 2) twice; p 2, [k 1, p 3, (k 1-b, p 1) 3 times; k 1-b, p 2, k 1], k 12, p 10, k 12. Rep bet [ ]s. (P 2, k 2) twice; p 2.

*Row 11:* (P 2, k 2) twice; p 2, [sl 1 to cable needle and hold in *back* of work, k 2, k 1-b from cable needle, (p 1, k 1-b) 4 times; sl 2 to cable needle and hold in *front* of work, p 1, k 2 from cable needle], k 10, p 2, sl 5 to cable needle and hold in *back* of work, k 5, k 5 from cable needle, p 2, k 10. Rep bet [ ]s. (P 2, k 2) twice; p 2.

*Row 12:* (K 2, p 2) twice; k 2, [p 2, (k 1-b, p 1) 5 times; p 2], (p 10, k 2) twice, p 10. Rep bet [ ]s. (K 2, p 2) twice; k 2.

*Row 13:* (K 2, p 2) twice; k 2, [sl 2 to cable needle and hold in *front* of work, p 1, k 2 from cable needle, (p 2, k 1-b) 4 times; sl 1 to cable needle and hold in *back* of work, k 2, p 1 from cable needle], (k 10, p 2) twice; k 10. Rep bet [ ]s. (K 2, p 2) twice; k 2.

*Row 14:* (P 2, k 2) twice; p 2, [k 1, p 3, (k 1-b, p 1) 3 times; k 1-b, p 2, k 1], (p 10, k 2) twice; p 10. Rep bet [ ]s. (P 2, k 2) twice; p 2.

*Row 15:* (P 2, k 2) twice; p 2, [p 1, sl 2 to cable needle and hold in *front* of work, p 1, k 2 from cable needle, (k 1-b, p 1) 3 times; sl 1 to cable needle and hold in *back* of work, k 2, p 1 from cable needle, p 1], (k 10, p 2) twice; k 10. Rep bet [ ]s. (P 2, k 2) twice; p 2.

*Row 16:* (K 2, p 2) twice; k 2, [k 2, p 2, (k 1-b, p 1) 3 times; p 2, k 2], (p 10, k 2) twice; p 10. Rep bet [ ]s. (K 2, p 2) twice; k 2.

*Row 17:* (K 2, p 2) twice; k 2, [p 2, sl 2 to cable needle and hold in *front* of work, p 1, k 2 from cable needle, (p 1, k 1-b) twice; sl 1 to cable needle and hold in *back* of work, k 2, p 1 from cable needle, p 2], (k 10, p 2) twice, k 10. Rep bet [ ]s. (K 2, p 2) twice; k 2.

*Row 18:* (P 2, k 2) twice; p 2, [k 3, p 3, k 1-b, p 1, k 1-b, p 2, k 3], (p 10, k 2) twice; p 10. Rep bet [ ]s. (P 2, k 2) twice; p 2.

*Row 19:* (P 2, k 2) twice; p 2, [p 3, sl 2 to cable needle and hold in *front* of work, p 1, k 2 from cable needle, k 1-b, p 1, sl 1 to cable needle and hold in *back* of work, k 2, p 1 from cable needle, p 3], (k 10, p 2) twice; k 10. Rep bet [ ]s. (P 2, k 2) twice; p 2.

*Row 20:* (K 2, p 2) twice; k 2, [k 4, p 2, k 1-b, p 3, k 4], (p 10, k 2) twice; p 10. Rep bet [ ]s. (K 2, p 2) twice; k 2.

*Row 21:* (K 2, p 2) twice; k 2, [p 4, sl 2 to cable needle and hold in *front* of work, p 1, k 2 from cable needle, sl 1 to cable needle and hold in *back* of work, k 2, p 1 from cable needle, p 4], p 12, sl 5 to cable needle and hold in *back* of work, k 5, k 5 from cable needle, p 12. Rep bet [ ]s. (K 2, p 2) twice; k 2.

Rep Rows 2–21 for pat until panel measures 72 inches, ending with row 2 of pat. Do not twist cable on final rep of Row 21. Make 3 more panels.

**To assemble the panels**

Lay two panels side by side with the right sides up. Working with 2 strands of yarn, sl st the panels tog as follows: **Insert hook under double strands of yarn at adjacent corners of panels, yo, draw yarn through strands of yarn and lp on hook—sl st made.**

Working at a relaxed tension to prevent puckering, continue to sl st up sides of panels, inserting hook under *single strand* of yarn at each edge every four rows. At end of panel, fasten off. Repeat the assembly instructions for the remaining two panels.

**For the fringe**

Cut 730 twelve-inch lengths of yarn. * Beg at corner, insert hook under two strands of yarn. Holding 5 strands of yarn tog, draw center of these strands back through the afghan, yo with doubled 5-strand and draw all ends through lp on hook. Pull to tighten knot. Rep from * every inch along both ends of afghan.

## Kids' Fisherman Knit Sweaters

Shown on page 62.
Directions are for Size Small (6–8); changes for Size Large (10–12) follow in parentheses.

**MATERIALS**
Bernat Berella: 16 (20) ounces of off-white
Sizes 5 and 7 knitting needles and Size 7 circular knitting needle for Size Small
Sizes 6 and 8 knitting needles and Size 8 circular knitting needle for Size Large, or sizes to obtain gauge given below
Cable needle; stitch holders
Jacket zipper
Size G aluminum crochet hook

**Abbreviations:** Page 217.
**Gauge:** Over double-seed st with Size 7 needles, 9 sts = 2 inches. Over double-seed st with Size 8 needles, 7 sts = 2 inches.

**INSTRUCTIONS**

*Note:* Zippered and pullover versions of the jackets shown are identical except for the fronts. Directions for both styles are included in the pattern below.

PATTERN A (double-seed st worked over an even number of sts)—*Rows 1 and 2:* K 1, * p 1, k 1. Rep from * across, ending with p 1.

*Rows 3 and 4:* P 1, * k 1, p 1. Rep from * across, ending with k 1. Rows 1-4 make up pat.

PATTERN B (double-seed st worked over an uneven number of sts)—*Row 1:* K 1, * p 1, k 1. Rep from * across.

*Rows 2 and 3:* P 1, * k 1, p 1. Rep from * across.

*Row 4:* K 1, * p 1, k 1. Rep from * across. Rows 1-4 make up pat.

PATTERN C (double twist over 5 sts)—*Row 1* (right side): * K in front of *second* st on left-hand needle, k in back of *first* st on left-hand needle, drop both sts from left-hand needle *, p 1, rep bet *s once more.

*Row 2:* P 2, k 1, p 2. Rows 1 and 2 make up pat.

PATTERN D (popcorn worked over 9 sts)—*Row 1:* P 2, **in next st k in front, in back, in front, in back, and in front—5 sts made in one st; drop st from left-hand needle; (using left-hand needle, pass second st over tip of right-hand needle and drop from needle) 4 times—popcorn made;** p 3, make another popcorn, p 2.

*Row 2:* K 9.

*Row 3:* P 4, work popcorn, p 4.

*Row 4:* K 9. Rows 1-4 make up pat.

PATTERN E (cable over 12 sts)—*Row 1:* P 2, sl next 2 sts to cable needle and hold in *front* of work, k next 2 sts, k 2 sts from cable needle; sl next 2 sts to cable needle and hold in *back* of work, k next 2 sts, k 2 sts from cable needle, p 2.

*Row 2:* K 2, p 8, k 2.

*Row 3:* P 2, k 8, p 2.

*Row 4:* Rep Row 2.

*Row 5:* P 2, sl next 2 sts to cable needle and hold in *back* of work, k next 2 sts, k 2 sts from cable needle; sl next 2 sts to cable needle and hold in *front* of work, k next 2 sts, k 2 sts from cable needle, p 2.

*Rows 6 and 7:* Rep Rows 2 and 3.

*Row 8:* Rep Row 2. Rows 1-8 make up pat.

BACK: With Size 5 (6) needles, cast on 80 sts. Work in k 1, p 1 ribbing for 2½ inches, inc 10 sts evenly spaced on last row—90 sts.

Establish pat as follows: Pat A over 4 sts; pat C over 5 sts; pat D over 9 sts; pat C over 5 sts; pat E over 12 sts; pat A over 20 sts; pat E over 12 sts; pat C over 5 sts; pat D over 9 sts; pat C over 5 sts; pat A over 4 sts. Keeping to pats as established, work even until total length from beg measures 11 (12½) inches, or desired length to underarm, ending with a wrong-side row.

ARMHOLE SHAPING: Bind off 4 sts at beg of next 2 rows. Work 2 rows even.

RAGLAN SHAPING—*Row 1:* K 1, sl 1, k 1, psso, work in pats to last 3 sts, k 2 tog, k 1.

*Row 2:* K 1, p 1, work in pat to last 2 sts, p 1, k 1. Rep Rows 1 and 2 16 times more, ending with a wrong-side row—48 sts.

*Next row:* K 1, sl 1, k 2 tog, psso, work to last 4 sts, k 3 tog, k 1.

*Following row:* Rep Row 2 of raglan shaping. Rep last 2 rows 5 times more—24 sts rem. Sl sts to holder.

PULLOVER FRONT: Work same as for Back until 48 sts rem, ending with a right-side row.

NECK SHAPING: K 1, p 1, work in pat for 15 sts, sl next 7 sts to a holder and sl following 7 sts to another holder; join a second ball of yarn and work to last 2 sts, p 1, k 1. Working both sides at the same time, continue to decrease at armholes as established *and at the same time* dec one st at neck edge every row until 3 sts rem.

*Next row:* K 1, p 2 tog. *Following row:* K 2 tog. Fasten off.

LEFT ZIPPERED FRONT: With Size 5 (6) needles, cast on 40 sts. Work in k 1, p 1 ribbing for 2½ inches, inc 5 sts evenly spaced across last row—45 sts.

Change to Size 7 (8) needle and establish pat as follows: Pat A over 4 sts; pat C over 5 sts; pat D over 9 sts; pat C over 5 sts; pat E over 12 sts; pat A over 10 sts.

Keeping to pats as established, work even until total length from beg equals that of Back to armhole, ending at armhole edge.

ARMHOLE SHAPING: Bind off 4 sts at beg of next row; work 3 rows even. Work raglan decs as for Back until 24 sts rem, ending with a wrong-side row.

*continued*

With right side facing, and continuing to work raglan decs, work across first 17 sts; sl next 7 sts to a holder; turn. Work one row even.

At each armhole edge continue to dec one st every other row and *at the same time* dec one st at neck edge every row until 3 sts rem.

*Next row:* K 1, p 2 tog.

*Following row:* K 2 tog; fasten off.

RIGHT ZIPPERED FRONT: Work same as for Left Front, reversing pats and shaping.

SLEEVES: With Size 5 (6) needle, cast on 42 sts. Work in k 1, p 1 ribbing for 2½ inches, inc 7 sts evenly spaced across last row—49 sts.

Establish pat as follows: Pat B over 15 sts; pat C over 5 sts; pat D over 9 sts; pat C over 5 sts; pat B over 15 sts.

Keeping to pats as established and working incs in seed st, inc 1 st each side every inch 5 times—59 sts. Work even until total length from beg measures 12½ (14) inches, or desired length to underarm, ending with a wrong-side row.

CAP SHAPING: Bind off 5 sts at beg of next 2 rows. Work 2 rows even. Work raglan armhole shaping as for Back; rep Rows 1 and 2 until 5 (7) sts rem. If necessary, work even over rem sts until sleeve armhole length equals that of Back. Sl rem sts to a holder.

Sew sleeves in place to front and back sections, then sew side and sleeve seams.

HOOD: With Size 7 (8) circular needle, cast on 5 sts. With right side of sweater facing and beg at center right front, work center 7 sts from holder, pick up and k 13 sts along right front neck edge, work 5 (7) sts from right sleeve, work 24 sts from holder at back of neck, inc 1 st on last st; work 5 (7) sts from left sleeve, pick up and k 13 sts along left front neck edge, work 7 sts from left front center holder; cast on 5 sts—85 (89) sts.

*Row 1* (wrong side): P 5 for casing, work in pat B across row to last 5 sts, p 5 for casing.

*Row 2:* K 5, work in pat to last 5 sts, k 5. Rep Rows 1 and 2 until total length of hood measures 10½ (12) inches.

With right side facing, work across 39 (41) sts, sl 1, k 2 tog, psso, place a marker on needle, k 1, place another marker on needle, k 3 tog, work across row in pat.

*Next row:* Work across row in pat to one st before marker, p 3, (sl markers), work across row in pat.

*Following row:* Work in pat to 3 sts before marker, sl 1, k 2 tog, psso, sl marker, k 1, sl marker, k 3 tog; complete row in pat.

Rep last 2 rows until 73 sts rem. Bind off.

With right sides facing, sew top of hood. Fold back casing at front edge and slip-stitch in place.

DRAWSTRING: With crochet hook and one strand of yarn, ch 200. Sk first ch and sl st in each rem ch across; fasten off. Draw cord through hood casing and knot each end.

PULLOVER POCKET: With Size 5 (6) needles, cast on 60 sts, work in k 1, p 1 ribbing for 3½ inches.

*Row 1:* K 1, sl 1, k 2 tog, psso, work in ribbing to last 4 sts, k 3 tog, k 1.

*Row 2:* K 1, p 1, work in ribbing to last 2 sts, p 1, k 1. Rep rows 1 and 2 until 16 sts rem. Bind off in ribbing. Center pocket on sweater front and sew in place.

LEFT POCKET, ZIPPERED JACKET: With Size 5 (6) needles, cast on 30 sts. Work in k 1, p 1 ribbing for 3½ inches.

*Row 1:* K 1, sl 1, k 2 tog, psso; complete row in ribbing.

*Row 2:* Work in ribbing to last 2 sts, p 1, k 1. Rep Rows 1 and 2 until 8 sts rem. Bind off.

RIGHT POCKET, ZIPPERED JACKET: Work as for Right Pocket until ribbing has been completed.

*Row 1:* Work in ribbing as established to last 4 sts, k 3 tog, k 1.

*Row 2:* K 1, p 1; complete row in ribbing. Rep Rows 1 and 2 until 8 sts rem. Bind off.

Sew the pockets into place; sew in the zipper.

## Knitted Ripple Afghan

Shown on page 64.
Finished size is 54x70 inches.

**MATERIALS**

Anny Blatt Sport Anny (100-gram skeins): 10 skeins No. 44 black, 9 skeins No. 1358 cobalt blue
36-inch-long Size 9 circular knitting needle, or size to obtain gauge given below
Size I aluminum crochet hook

**Abbreviations:** Page 217.
**Gauge:** 7 sts = 2 inches.

**INSTRUCTIONS**

**For the afghan**

With black, cast on 227 sts. *Row 1* (right side): K 3, sl 1, k 1, psso, * k 19, sl 2 as if to k, k 1, p2sso. (*P2sso = pass 2 sl sts over.*) Rep from * to last 24 sts, ending with k 19, k 2 tog, k 3.

*Row 2:* K 3, p 10; * **insert right-hand tip of needle under running thread before next st, leave lp on right-hand tip of needle—make 1 (M 1) made;** p 1, M1, p 19. Rep from * across to last 14 sts, ending with M 1, p 1, M 1, p 10, k 3. Rep Rows 1–2 for pat.

* Work a total of 14 rows with black. Change to blue and work 14 rows of pat. Rep from * until 10 black stripes have been worked. Bind off.

**For the edging**

With crochet hook, blue, and right side facing, attach yarn at right-hand edge of 1 short end of afghan. Ch 2, hdc in each of first 3 sts; hdc across, making (hdc, ch 2, hdc) at "peaks" and sk 2 sts at "valleys," ending with 3 hdc in last 3 sts; ch 2, turn. Work another row of hdc similarly, working (hdc, **ch 4, sl st in fourth ch from hook—picot made,** hdc) in each ch-2 sp. *At the same time,* sk 2 hdc at "valleys." Fasten off. Rep for other short end of afghan.

*Note:* To adjust width of afghan, add or subtract a multiple of 22 sts. Establish pat as given in Row 1.

# Woman's Granny Square Pullover

Shown on page 65.

Directions are for Size Small [8–10]; changes for Size Medium [12–14] and Size Large [16] follow in brackets. Finished bust = 33¾ [37½, 40] inches.

**MATERIALS**

Coats and Clark Red Heart sport yarn: 10 (11, 12) ounces of No. 111 eggshell; 1 skein each of No. 905 red, No. 588 amethyst, No. 360 wood brown, No. 686 paddy green, No. 251 vibrant orange, No. 225 daffodil, and No. 845 royal blue

Size I aluminum crochet hook, or size to obtain gauge below

**Abbreviations:** Page 211.

**Gauge:** With 2 strands yarn held tog, 3 hdc = 1 inch; 2 hdc rows = 1 inch. Each motif measures 3⅜ (3¾, 4) inches square.

**INSTRUCTIONS**

*Note:* Sweater is worked with 2 strands of yarn held tog throughout. **Instructions within brackets [ ] are for sizes; instructions within parentheses ( ) are for pattern repeats.**

FRONT, Motif (make 4): Beg at center with 1 strand eggshell and 1 strand orange held tog, ch 4; join with sl st to form ring. *Rnd 1:* Ch 5 [6, 6], * make 3 hdc [3 dc, 3 dc] in ring, ch 3 for corner. Rep from * twice more; 2 hdc [2 dc, 2 dc] in ring; join with sl st to 2nd [3rd, 3rd] ch of beg ch-5 [ch-6, ch-6].

*Rnd 2:* Sl st in first corner sp, ch 3, in same sp make 2 dc, ch 3, and 3 dc, (ch 1, in next sp make 3 dc, ch 3, and 3 dc) 3 times; ch 1; join with sl st to top of beg ch-3. Fasten off.

*Rnd 3:* Join 2 strands eggshell to any corner sp, ch 1 [1, 2], * in corner sp make 5 sc [5 sc, 5 hdc]; sc [sc, hdc] in each st to next corner sp including the ch-1 st. Rep from * around; join with sl st to first sc [sc, hdc]. Fasten off.

Make 19 more motifs with the following colors: 4 motifs with 1 strand eggshell and 1 strand amethyst held tog; 3 motifs with eggshell and royal blue; 3 motifs with eggshell and daffodil; 3 motifs with eggshell and red; 3 motifs with eggshell and wood brown; and 3 motifs with eggshell and paddy green.

Arranging colors at random, make a strip of 5 motifs; join by sewing through the *back loops only.* Make 3 more strips of 5 motifs each. Sew the 4 strips tog. Make last strip with 3 motifs and sew it to center 3 motifs of previous strip.

SHAPED MOTIF FOR LEFT ARMHOLE*:* With eggshell and contrast color, ch 4; join with sl st to form ring.

*Rnd 1:* Ch 5 [6, 6], * 3 hdc [3 dc, 3 dc] in ring, ch 3. Rep from * once more, 1 hdc [1 dc, 1 dc] in ring. Fasten off; do not turn.

*Rnd 2:* Join same colors to 2nd [3rd, 3rd] ch of ch-5 [ch-6, ch-6] at beg of previous rnd; ch 3; in ch-3 lp formed by rem 3 chs of ch-5 [ch-6, ch-6] make 1 dc, ch 3 and 3 dc; ch 1; in next ch-3 sp make 3 dc, ch 3, and 3 dc; ch 1, 3 dc in next ch-3 sp, dc in last hdc [dc, dc]. Fasten off; do not turn.

*Rnd 3:* Join 2 strands eggshell to ch-3 at beg of previous rnd, ch 1 [ch 1, ch 2], sc [sc, hdc] in same place as joining; working around the motif, make 5 sc [5 sc, 5 hdc] in each ch-3 lp, sc [sc, hdc] in each dc and ch-1 sp to within last st. Work 3 sc [3 sc, 3 hdc] in last st. Do not turn; sc evenly across shaped (armhole) edge, being careful to keep work flat. Join to beg sc [sc, hdc]. Fasten off; sew in place.

SHAPED MOTIF FOR RIGHT ARMHOLE*:* With eggshell and contrast color, work as for other shaped motif until Rnd 1 has been completed.

*Rnd 2:* Join same color strands to 2nd [3rd, 3rd] ch of ch-5 [ch-6, ch-6]; ch 3, in ch-3 sp formed by rem 3 chs of ch-5 [ch-6, ch-6] make 3 dc, ch 1; in next ch-3 sp make 3 dc, ch 3 and 3 dc, ch 1, in next ch-3 sp make 3 dc, ch 3, 1 dc; dc in next dc. Fasten off. Do not turn.

*Rnd 3:* Work as for Rnd 3 of Shaped Motif for Left Armhole and sew in place.

YOKE*:* With right side of Front facing, join 2 strands of eggshell to first st at upper right-hand corner.

*Row 1:* Ch 2, make 39 [41, 46] hdc evenly spaced across top edge; ch 2, turn.

*Row 2:* Hdc in each hdc across; ch 2, turn. Rep Row 2 until total length of Front measures 19½ [21½, 22½] inches; end with a wrong-side row; ch 2, turn.

*continued*

LEFT NECK SHAPING: *Row 1:* (right side) Work first 11 [12, 13] hdc, **yo, draw up lp in each of next 2 hdc, yo, draw through all lps on hook—hdc-dec made;** do not work over rem sts; ch 2, turn.

*Row 2:* Work 1 hdc-dec over first 2 hdc; hdc in each hdc across row—11 [12, 13] hdc. *For Size Large only:* Work 2 rows even. *For all sizes:* ch 1, turn.

SHOULDER SHAPING: Sc in first 3 [4, 4] hdc, hdc in next 8 [8, 9] hdc. Fasten off.

RIGHT NECK SHAPING: With right side facing, sk next 13 [14, 16] hdc on last long row worked; join 2 strands eggshell to next hdc.

*Row 1:* Ch 2, dec 1 hdc over same st where yarn was joined and next hdc, hdc in each st across; ch 2, turn.

*Row 2:* Work in pat to last 2 hdc, dec 1 hdc over last 2 hdc—11 [12, 13] hdc; ch 2, turn. *For Size Large only:* Work 2 rows even. *For all sizes:* ch 2, turn.

SHOULDER SHAPING: Hdc in first 8 [8, 9] hdc, sc in each rem hdc. Fasten off.

BACK: Beg at lower edge with 2 strands eggshell held tog, ch 53 [58, 62] having 3 ch sts per inch.

*Row 1* (right side): Hdc in third ch from hook and in each ch across—51 [56, 60] hdc; ch 2, turn. (Do not count ch-2 as a st.)

*Row 2:* Hdc in each hdc; ch 2, turn. Rep Row 2 until total length measures same as Front to beg of shaped edge of armhole motif.

ARMHOLE SHAPING: *Row 1:* Sl st in first 2 hdc; ch 2, hdc-dec over next 2 sts; hdc in each hdc to last 4 hdc, hdc-dec over next 2 sts; do not work over rem hdc—45 [50, 54] hdc; ch 2, turn.

Keeping to pat, dec 1 hdc at each end of next 3 [4, 4] rows. Work even over 39 [42, 46] hdc until length past beg of armhole shaping measures is same as Front to beg of shoulder shaping; ch 1, turn.

SHOULDER SHAPING: Sc in first 3 [4, 4] hdc, hdc in next 8 [8, 9] hdc. Fasten off. Sk next 17 [18, 20] hdc for back of neck, join 2 strands held tog to next hdc, ch 2, hdc in same place where yarn was joined and in next 7 [7, 8] hdc, sc in rem 3 [4, 4] hdc. Fasten off.

SLEEVES: Beg at lower edge with 2 strands eggshell, ch 29 [31, 34].

*Row 1* (right side): Hdc in third ch from hook, and in each ch across; ch 2, turn. Work in hdc as for Back over 27 [29, 32] hdc until 4 rows are worked; ch 2, turn.

*Next row:* **2 hdc in first hdc—inc made,** hdc in each hdc to last hdc, inc in last hdc; ch 2, turn. Work 3 rows even. Rep last 4 rows 5 times more—39 [41, 44] hdc. Work even until total length measures 15 [16, 16] inches.

TOP SHAPING, *Row 1:* Rep Row 1 of Armhole Shaping of Back. Working in hdc, dec 1 hdc at each end of every row 8 [9, 10] times—17 [17, 18] hdc; ch 1, turn.

*Last row:* Sc in first hdc, hdc-dec over next 2 hdc, hdc in each hdc to last 3 hdc, hdc-dec next 2 hdc; sc in last hdc. Fasten off.

Block. Sew sleeve, side, and shoulder seams. Sew in sleeves, easing to fit.

LOWER BACK AND FRONT RIBBING: Beg at narrow edge with 2 strands of eggshell, ch 7. *Row 1:* Sc in second ch from hook and in each ch across—6 sc; ch 1, turn.

*Row 2:* Sc in back lp of each sc across; ch 1, turn. Rep Row 2 until ribbing when slightly stretched measures 30 [33½, 36] inches. Fasten off. Sew the narrow edges tog. Sew ribbing in place, easing the pullover to fit.

SLEEVE RIBBING (make 2): Work as for Lower Ribbing of Back for 7 [7½, 8½] inches. Fasten off. Sew narrow edges tog. Sew in place, easing sleeve to fit.

NECKBAND: Work as for lower ribbing until neckband fits neck edge. Fasten off. Sew narrow edges tog; sew to neckline.

## Child's Granny Square Pullover

Shown on page 65.

Directions are for Size 4; changes for Sizes 6, 8, and 10 follow in brackets. Chest = 23 [24, 26, 28] inches.

**MATERIALS**

Coats and Clark Red Heart sport yarn (1¾-ounce skeins): 6 [7, 7, 8] skeins of No. 111 eggshell, 1 skein *each* of No. 905 red, No. 588 amethyst, No. 360 wood brown, No. 686 paddy green, No. 251 vibrant orange, No. 225 daffodil, and No. 845 royal blue

Size I aluminum crochet hook, or size to obtain gauge below

**Abbreviations:** Page 211.

**Gauge:** With 2 strands yarn held tog, 3 hdc = 1 inch; 2 hdc rows = 1 inch. Each motif measures 2¼ [2½, 2¼, 2½] inches.

**INSTRUCTIONS**

*Note:* Sweater is worked with 2 strands of yarn held tog throughout. **Instructions given in brackets [ ] are for sizes; instructions within parentheses ( ) are for pattern repeats.**

FRONT, Motif: Beg at center with 1 strand eggshell and 1 strand of any contrasting color held tog, ch 4; join with sl st to form ring.

*Rnd 1:* Ch 2 [3, 2, 3]; make 2 hdc [2 dc, 2 hdc, 2 dc] in ring; * ch 3 for corner, 3 hdc [3 dc, 3 hdc, 3 dc] in ring. Rep from * twice more, ch 3 for corner; join with sl st to top of ch-2 [ch-3, ch-2, ch-3]. Fasten off.

*Rnd 2:* Join 2 strands eggshell to any corner sp, ch 1, * 5 sc in corner sp, sc in next 3 sts. Rep from * around; join with sl st to first sc. Fasten off. Working the motif as before, make 22 [22, 33, 33] more motifs using 1 strand of eggshell and 1 strand of any contrasting color held tog. Arranging colors at random, make a strip of 5 [5, 6, 6] motifs; join by sewing through *back lps only.* Make 3 [3, 4, 4] more strips. Sew strips tog. Sew rem 3 [3, 4, 4] motifs tog for last strip, then sew last strip to center 3 [3, 4, 4] motifs of previous strip.

SHAPED MOTIF FOR LEFT ARMHOLE: With 1 strand eggshell and 1 strand contrasting color, ch 4; join with sl st to form ring.

*Rnd 1:* Ch 2 [3, 2, 3]; in ring make 6 hdc [6 dc, 4 hdc, 4 dc]; ch 3 for corner, and 4 hdc [4 dc, 4 hdc, 4 dc]. Fasten off; do not turn.

*Rnd 2:* Join 2 strands eggshell to top of ch-2 [ch-3, ch-2, ch-3] at beg of previous row, ch 1, sc in same place as joining, sc in each st to next corner sp, 5 sc in corner sp, sc in each st to within last st, 3 sc in last st. Work sc evenly spaced along shaped edge, being careful to keep work flat; join with sl st to first sc. Fasten off; sew in place.

SHAPED MOTIF FOR RIGHT ARMHOLE: With eggshell and contasting color, ch 4; join with sl st to form ring.

*Row 1:* Ch 2 [3, 2, 3], in ring make 3 hdc [3 dc, 3 hdc, 3 dc], ch 3 for corner and 7 hdc [7 dc, 5 hdc, 5 dc]. Fasten off. Do not turn. Complete as for Rnd 2 of other shaped motif and sew in place.

YOKE: With right side of Front facing, join 2 strands eggshell to first st at upper right-hand corner.

*Row 1:* Ch 2, make 27 [30, 31, 35] hdc evenly spaced across; ch 2, turn.

*Row 2:* Hdc in each hdc across, ch 2, turn. Rep Row 2 until total length measures 12½ [14, 16, 17½] inches; end with a wrong-side row; ch 2, turn.

LEFT NECK SHAPING: *Row 1:* Work in pat across first 7 [8, 8, 9] hdc, **yo, draw up lp in each of next 2 hdc, yo, draw through all lps on hook—hdc-dec made;** do not work over rem sts; ch 2, turn.

*Row 2:* Work hdc-dec over first 2 hdc, complete row in pat—7 [8, 8, 9] hdc; ch 1, turn.

SHOULDER SHAPING: Sc in first 3 hdc, hdc in next 4 [5, 5, 6] hdc. Fasten off.

RIGHT NECK SHAPING: With right side facing sk next 9 [10, 11, 13] hdc on last long row worked, join 2 strands of eggshell to next hdc.

*Row 1:* Ch 2, work hdc-dec over same st where yarn was joined and next hdc; complete row in pat; ch 2, turn.

*Row 2:* Work in pat to last 2 hdc, work hdc-dec over last 2 hdc—7 [8, 8, 9] hdc; ch 2, turn.

SHOULDER SHAPING: Hdc in first 4 [5, 5, 6] hdc, sc in each rem hdc. Fasten off.

BACK: Beg at lower edge with 2 strands eggshell held tog, ch 37 [40, 43, 45] having 3 ch sts per inch.

*Row 1* (right side): Hdc in third ch from hook and in each ch across—35 [38, 41, 43] hdc; ch 2, turn. (Do not count ch-2 as hdc.)

*Row 2:* Hdc in each hdc across; ch 2, turn.

Rep Row 2 until length measures same as Front to beginning of shaped edge of armhole motif.

ARMHOLE SHAPING: *Row 1:* Sl st in first st, ch 2, hdc-dec over next 2 hdc, hdc in each hdc to last 3 hdc, hdc-dec over next 2 hdc—31 [34, 37, 39] hdc; do not work over last hdc; ch 2, turn. Keeping to pat work hdc-dec at each end of next 2 [2, 3, 3] rows—27 [30, 31, 33] hdc. Work even until total length past beg of armholes measures same as Front to beginning of shoulder shaping; ch 1, turn.

SHOULDER SHAPING: Sc in first 3 hdc, hdc in next 4 [5, 5, 6] hdc. Fasten off. Sk next 13 [14, 15, 17] hdc for back of neck, join 2 strands to next hdc, ch 2, hdc in same place where yarn was joined and in next 3 [4, 4, 5] hdc, sc in rem hdc. Fasten off.

SLEEVES: Beg at lower edge with 2 strands eggshell held tog, ch 25 [27, 29, 31]. Work in pat as for Back over 23 [25, 27, 29] hdc for 4 rows. Work 2 hdc in next hdc, work across in pat to last hdc, work 2 hdc in last hdc—1 hdc inc at each end; ch 2, turn—25 [27, 29, 31] hdc. Rep the inc at each and every 6th [6th, 8th, 8th] row twice—29 [31, 33, 35] hdc. Work even until total length measures 9½ [11, 12, 13] inches.

TOP SHAPING: *Row 1:* Rep Row 1 of Armhole Shaping of Back; ch 2, turn—25 [27, 29, 31] hdc.

*Rows 2–3:* Work hdc-dec over first 2 hdc, hdc-dec over next 2 hdc, work in pat to last 4 sts, (hdc-dec over next 2 hdc) twice; ch 2, turn—21 [23, 25, 27] hdc. Keeping to pat, work hdc-dec at each end of every row 5 [6, 7, 8] times—11 hdc; ch 1, turn.

*Last row:* Sc in first hdc, work hdc-dec over next 2 hdc, hdc in each hdc to last 3 hdc, work hdc-dec over next 2 hdc; sc in last hdc. Fasten off.

Pin to measurements, dampen and leave to dry. Sew the sleeve, side, and shoulder seams. Sew in the sleeves.

*continued*

LOWER RIBBING: Beg at narrow edge with 2 strands eggshell held tog, ch 5.

*Row 1:* Sc in second ch from hook and in each ch across; ch 1, turn.

*Row 2:* Sc in back lp of each sc across; ch 1, turn. Rep Row 2 until the ribbing, slightly stretched, measures 22 [23, 25, 27] inches. Fasten off. Sew narrow edges tog. Sew ribbing in place, easing lower edge of pullover to fit.

SLEEVE RIBBING: Work as for Lower Ribbing until ribbing when slightly stretched measures 6 [7, 8, 8½] inches. Fasten off. Sew narrow edges tog; sew in place, easing the sleeve to fit.

NECKBAND: Work as for Lower Ribbing until the neckband when slightly stretched fits around neck edge. Fasten off. Sew narrow edges tog; sew to neckline.

## Fair Isle Vest

Shown on page 66.

Directions are for Size Small (6–8); changes for Size Medium (10–12) and Size Large (14–16) follow in parentheses. Bust = 36¼ (37¾, 40) inches.

**FAIR ISLE VEST**

**Pat. 1**

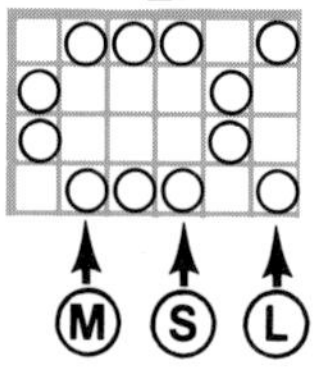


◘ **Rep. 1-B**
**2-F**
**3-E**

**Pat. 2**

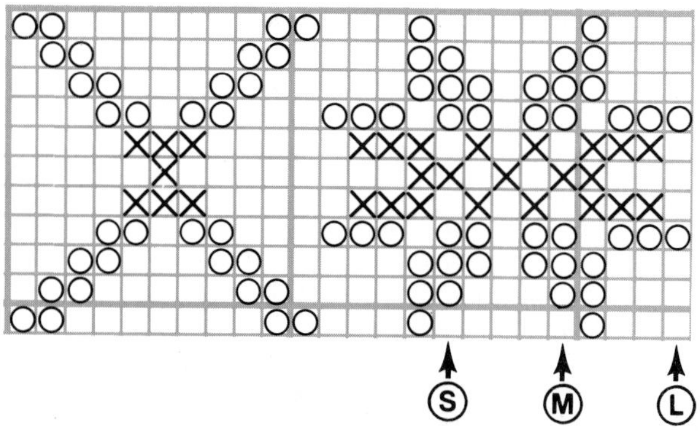


◘ **Rep. 1-C**
**2-B**
**3-F**

☒ **Rep. 1-D**
**2-D**
**3-B**

**Pat. 3**

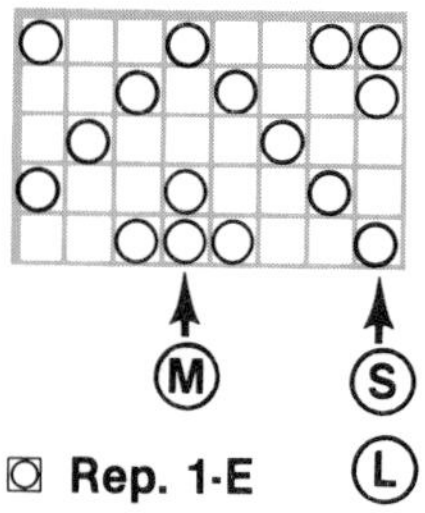


◘ **Rep. 1-E**
**2-C**
**3-D**

**Pat. 4**

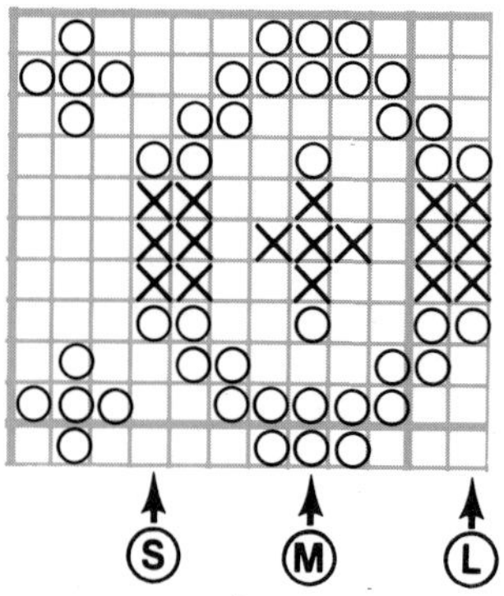


◘ **Rep. 1-F**
**2-E**
**3-C**

☒ **Rep. 1-B**
**2-F**
**3-E**

**Pat. 5**

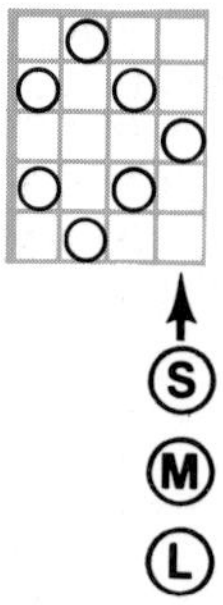


◘ **Rep. 1-D**
**2-B**
**3-F**

**Pat. 6**

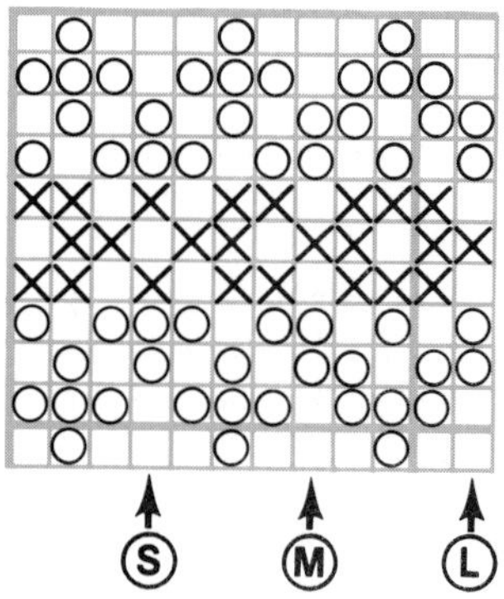


◘ **Rep. l-C**
**2-C**
**3-B**

☒ **Rep. 1-E**
**2-D**
**3-D**

**1 Square = 1 Stitch**

**MATERIALS**

Chantelaine Shetfine yarn (50-gram balls): 3 balls of No. 014 dark gray (color A); 1 ball *each* of No. 002 camel (color B), No. 011 maroon (color C), No. 001 off-white (color D), No. 012 rose (color E), and No. 031 taupe (color F)

Sizes 3 and 5 knitting needles, or size to obtain gauge below

**Abbreviations:** Page 217.

**Gauge:** With larger needles over st st, 15 sts = 2 inches; 17 rows = 2 inches.

**INSTRUCTIONS**

BACK: With smaller needles and A, cast on 112 (120, 128) sts. Work in k 1, p 1 ribbing for 2¾ inches. Change to larger needles and work in st st (k 1 row, p 1 row) for 4 rows, inc 8 (8, 8) sts on first row—120 (128, 136) sts.

Making incs as directed below, referring to charts, *opposite,* and keeping to st st as established, work each rep of charts in colors as indicated, working 2 rows of A bet each pattern and 3 rows of A bet pat 6 and pat 1. Inc 1 st each end every 10th (12th, 12th) row 6 (7, 3) times; then every 11th (0, 13th) row 2 (0, 4) times—136 (142, 150) sts. Work even until total length measures 13½ (14, 14½) inches, ending with a wrong-side row.

ARMHOLE SHAPING: Bind off 11 (12, 13) sts at beg of next 2 rows. Dec 1 st each end every other row 7 (8, 7) times, then every third row 4 (2, 4) times and every fourth row 1 (2, 2) times—90 (94, 98) sts.

SHOULDER SHAPING: When length from beg of armhole shaping measures 7½ (8, 8½) inches end with a wrong-side row. Bind off 7 sts at beg of next 6 rows. Sl rem 48 (52, 56) sts to holder for Back neck.

FRONT: Work as for Back to armhole ending with wrong-side row and placing marker in center of row.

ARMHOLE SHAPING: Work same as Back until 14 rows following armhole bind-off sts are completed; end with a wrong-side row.

Continuing to shape armholes as for Back, beg neck shaping as follows: Work to 2 sts before marker, k 2 tog, remove marker, k 2 tog, work to end of row.

Working each side separately, dec 1 st at neck edge every other row 22 (24, 26) times, then every third row 2 (2, 2) times.

When length from beg of armhole shaping measures same as Back to shoulder, bind off 7 sts at armhole edge 3 (3, 3) times. Rep for other side, reversing shaping.

ARMBAND FINISHING: Seam shoulders. With right side facing, smaller needles, and A, pick up 68 (73, 78) sts from armhole to shoulder and same number from shoulder to other armhole—136 (146, 156) sts.

Work in k 1, p 1 ribbing for 10 rows. Bind off in ribbing.

NECKBAND FINISHING: With right side facing, smaller needles, and A, pick up 47 (51, 54) sts along right neck edge, work 48 (52, 56) sts from back neck holder. Pick up 47 (51, 54) sts along left neck edge—142 (154, 164) sts. Do not join.

Work in ribbing of k 1, p 1 for 10 rows. Bind off in ribbing. At center front place edge of right neckband over left neckband and seam edges of both to sides of V. Sew side seams.

## Argyle Cardigan

Shown on page 67.

Directions are for Size Small (40); changes for Sizes Medium (42) and Large (44) are in parentheses. Chest = 42½ (44½, 46½) inches.

**MATERIALS**

Unger Skol (1.6-ounce balls): 12 (13, 14) balls of color A (MC), 1 ball of color B (diamond), 1 ball of color C (crossbars )

Sizes 7 and 9 knitting needles, or size to obtain gauge given below

Size 7 circular needle

4¾-inch-diameter buttons

3 knitting bobbins

**Abbreviations:** Page 217.

**Gauge:** With larger needles over st st, 4 sts = 1 inch; 5 rows = 1 inch.

**INSTRUCTIONS**

BACK: With smaller needles and MC, cast on 84 (88, 92) sts. Work in k 1, p 1 ribbing for 1¾ inches. Change to larger needles and st st (k 1 row, p 1 row), working even until total length measures 16 (16½, 17) inches.

ARMHOLE SHAPING: Bind off 3 sts at beg of next 2 rows. Dec 1 st each end of every other row 4 (5, 6) times—70 (72, 74) sts. Work even until the length from the beg of the armhole shaping measures 10 (10½, 11) inches.

SHOULDER SHAPING: Bind off 6 sts at beg of next 4 (2, 2) rows. Bind off 7 sts at beg of next 2 (4, 4) rows. Sl rem 32 (32, 34) sts to holder for Back neck.

RIGHT FRONT: With smaller needles and MC, cast on 40 (42, 44) sts. Work in k 1, p 1 ribbing for 1¾ inches. Change to larger needles and work 2 rows of st st. Wind 2 bobbins with MC and 1 with B.

Beg diamond shape as follows: *Row 1:* K 19 (20, 21) with MC, 1 (1, 1) with B, 20 (21, 22) with MC.

*Row 2:* P 20 (21, 22) with MC, 1 (1, 1) with B, 19 (20, 21) with MC.

*Row 3:* K 18 (19, 20) with MC, 3 (3, 3) with B, 19 (20, 21) with MC.

*continued*

*Row 4:* P 19 (20, 21) with MC, 3 (3, 3) with B, 18 (19, 20) with MC.

Continue in this way, working 1 more st in B at each side of the diamond until there are 31 sts in B; end with a wrong-side row.

Then work 1 less st in B at each side of the diamond until there is 1 (1, 1) B st remaining; end with a wrong-side row. Break off all bobbins. Continue with ball of MC.

NECK SHAPING: Continue working in pat and *at the same time,* when the total length measures 12 inches, dec 1 st every fourth row at the Front edge 14 (14, 15) times.

**ARGYLE CARDIGAN**

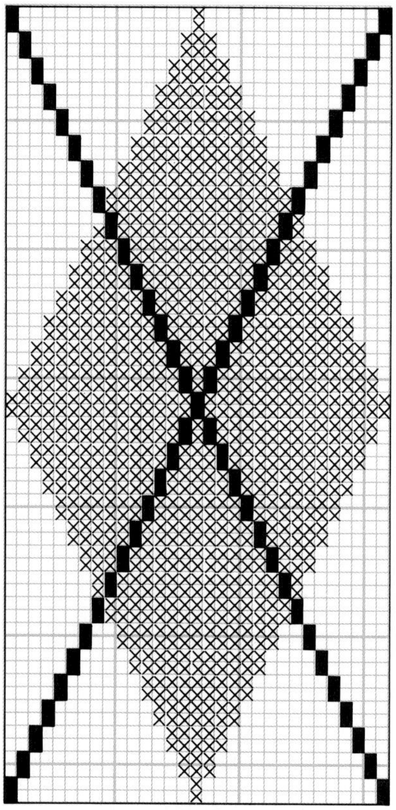

☐ A  1 Square = 1 Stitch
☒ B
■ C

ARMHOLE SHAPING: Continue working in pat and neck shaping and *at the same time,* when total length measures 16 (16½, 17) inches ending with a right-side row, bind off 3 sts at beg of next row for armhole. Dec 1 st at armhole edge every other row 4 (5, 6) times—19 (20, 20) sts.

SHOULDER SHAPING: When length from beg of armhole measures 10 (10½, 11) inches, end with right-side row and bind off 6 sts at beg of every other row 2 (1, 1) times. Bind off 7 sts at beg of every other row 1 (2, 2) time.

LEFT FRONT: Work as for Right Front, reversing shaping.

SLEEVES: With smaller needles and MC, cast on 36 (38, 40) sts. Work in k 1, p 1 ribbing for 2½ inches, inc 10 (12, 14) sts evenly across last row—46 (50, 54) sts.

Change to larger needles and st st. Inc 1 st at each end every 1½ inches 10 (10, 10) times—66 (70, 74) sts. Work even until the total length measures 19½ (20, 20½) inches, ending with a wrong-side row.

TOP SHAPING: Bind off 3 (4, 5) sts at beg of next 2 rows. Dec 1 st at each end of every other row 15 (16, 17) times. Bind off 3 (3, 3) sts at the beg of the next 6 rows. Bind off rem 12 sts.

FINISHING: Following chart, *left,* work crossbars in C using duplicate sts (see *opposite* for an explanation and diagram of this stitch). Seam shoulders.

NECKBAND: With the right side of the work facing, and using smaller needles and MC, beg at lower edge of Right Front and pick up 154 (158, 164) sts along the Right Front edge, work 32 (32, 34) sts from back neck holder, pick up 155 (159, 165) sts along the Left Front edge—341 (349, 363) sts.

* P 1, k 1. Rep from * across, ending with p 1. Work in ribbing as established for 2 rows more, ending at lower Right Front edge.

Work in ribbing to last 57 sts, * bind off 3 sts, (1 st rem on right needle) work next 13 sts in rib. Rep from * twice more, bind off 3 sts, (1 st rem on right needle) work last 2 sts in ribbing.

*Next row:* Work in ribbing, casting on 3 sts over the bind-off sts of previous row, continue in ribbing to the end of the row. Work 2 more rows in ribbing, then bind off in ribbing. Sew the side and sleeve seams. Sew on 4 buttons.

# Basket Weave Pullovers

Shown on pages 68–69.
Directions are for a sweater sized to fit a 32-inch chest or bust; changes for a sweater sized to fit a 36-, 40-, and 44-inch chest or bust follow in parentheses.

**MATERIALS**

Tahki Donegal Tweed (100-gram skeins) in the color of your choice: 6 (6, 7, 8) skeins

Sizes 6 and 8 knitting needles, or size to obtain gauge given below

**Abbreviations:** Page 217.

**Gauge:** Over pat st with larger needles, 4 sts = 1 inch; 6 rows = 1 inch.

**INSTRUCTIONS**

PATTERN ST— ***Rows 1 and 3* (right side): P 5, * k 3, p 5. Rep from * across.**

***Rows 2 and 4:* K 5, * p 3, k 5. Rep from * across.**

***Rows 5 and 7:* K 4, p 5, * k 3, p 5. Rep from * across, ending with k 4.**

***Rows 6 and 8:* P 4, k 5, * p 3, k 5. Rep from * across, ending with p 4.**

BACK: With smaller needles, cast on 55 (65, 75, 83) sts. Work even in garter st (k every row) for 2½ (2½, 3½, 3½) inches, inc 14 (12, 10, 10) sts evenly spaced across last row—69 (77, 85, 93) sts.

Change to larger needles and work even in pat st until the total length measures 13 (13, 17, 18) inches, or desired length to underarm, ending on the wrong side with Row 6 of the pat. Mark the ends for underarm.

ARMHOLE SHAPING: Keeping to pat, bind off 8 sts at beg of next 2 rows—53 (61, 69, 77) sts. Work even until total length above markers measures 7 (7½, 7½, 8) inches, ending on wrong side with Row 6.

SHOULDER SHAPING: Bind off 5 (6, 7, 7) sts at beg of next 4 (4, 6, 6) rows; then bind off 7 (7, 0, 2) sts at beg of next 2 rows. Sl rem 19 (23, 27, 31) sts to holder for back of neck.

FRONT: Work same as for Back until total length past armhole markers measures 4½ (5, 6½, 6½) inches, ending on right side with Row 3—53 (61, 69, 77) sts.

FRONT NECK SHAPING: Work across first 19 (23, 26, 28) sts and sl sts to holder for right side of neck; work center 15 (15, 17, 21) sts for front of neck and sl sts to holder; complete row in pat. Work left side only, dec one st at neck edge every other row 3 (4, 5, 6) times—16 (19, 21, 22) sts. Work even until total length past the armhole markers equals that of the Back, ending at shoulder edge.

FRONT SHOULDER SHAPING: Bind off 5 (6, 7, 7) sts at beg of next row; work one row even. Rep last 2 rows 1 (1, 2, 2) time more. Bind off rem sts.

Sl sts on right side to needle and work the right neck and shoulder shaping to correspond to left side.

NECKBAND: Sew left shoulder seam. Sl sts from back neck holder to needle; pick up and k 12 (12, 14, 16) sts along left neck edge; sl sts from front neck holder to needle; pick up and k 12 (12, 14, 16) sts along right neck edge—58 (62, 72, 84) sts. Work even in garter sts for 6 rows. Bind off loosely as to k.

SLEEVES: With smaller needles, cast on 27 (27, 36, 36) sts. Work even in garter st for 2½ (2½, 3½, 3½) inches, inc 18 (18, 17, 17) sts evenly spaced across the last row. Change to larger needles and pat. Work even for 8 (8, 10, 10) rows. *Next row* (inc row): Inc one st each side of next row. Rep inc row every 8 (8, 10, 10)th row 7 times—61 (61, 69, 69) sts. Work even until total length of sleeve measures 16 (16, 19, 19) inches, or desired length to underarm, ending on wrong side with Row 8. Bind off in pat.

FINISHING: Sew shoulder and sleeve seams, leaving 2 inches open at top. Sew remaining 2 inches of sleeve to bind-off sts of underarms. Sew sleeves into the armholes. Sew side seams.

## Duplicate-Stitch Embroidery

One way to give your knitted work a new look is to use duplicate-stitch embroidery. This stitch is used to duplicate the shape of each knitted stitch so the finished design looks as if it's knitted into the fabric.

Duplicate stitch can be used in many ways. For example, you can turn a plain knitted sweater front into an argyle design or add an initial to a sweater for a monogram that looks knitted in.

Duplicate-stitch embroidery is widely used to simulate Fair Isle knitting which is characterized by multicolor motifs that are repeated across sweater yokes and sleeves to form a patterned band. Traditionally, each color of yarn is carried across the back of the work and knitted as it's needed. Using duplicate stitch, however, you can knit the entire piece with just the background color and add the motifs after the sweater is complete.

To work duplicate stitch, thread a tapestry needle with the yarn needed for the design. Hold the work's right side toward you.

Bring the needle through the designated stitch from back (wrong side) to front. Following the shape of the stitch, insert the needle through and around the back of the stitch *directly above* and back to the front of the work. Then re-insert the needle through to the back of the work at the point where the stitch was begun, as shown in the diagram.

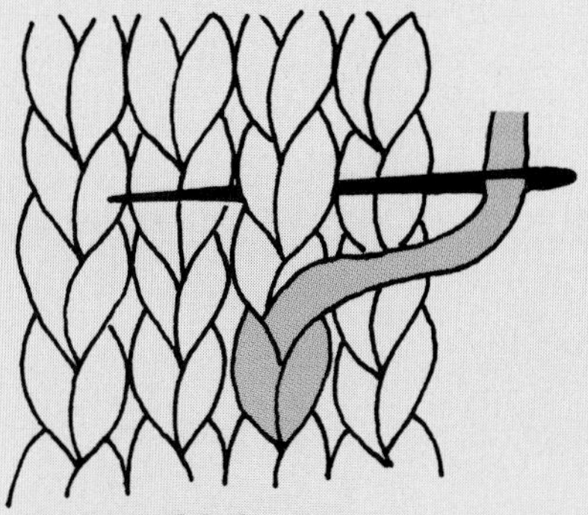

**Duplicate Stitch**

*Knitting and Crocheting the Classics*

# ELEGANT HEIRLOOMS FOR YOUR HOME

***Love of the traditional and delight in the handmade is the spirit that inspires beautiful heirloom crafts. The tablecloths and coverlets that grace this section are stitchery masterpieces that you'll be proud to make and enjoy year after year.***

Make teatime or anytime a festive occasion with this linen cloth embellished with lacy fancywork.

Silhouettes worked in filet crochet highlight the 8½-inch-wide edging. With the border, this cloth is 50 inches square, but you easily can adjust the size to fit your own table by adding or subtracting motifs. Directions begin on page 94.

# ELEGANT HEIRLOOMS

Whatever the occasion—be it impromptu midmorning coffee or an elegant repast for a wedding reception—there's no nicer way to set the table than with a beautiful cloth you've made yourself. The romantic cloth shown here is reminiscent of the lacy designs of days gone by and is sure to lend an air of nostalgia to any type of entertaining.

Dainty threads, delicate colors, and the lavish use of lacy stitches combine to create this contemporary tablecloth that's as lovely as any you might find on a foray to your favorite antique shop. You can stitch this stunning tabletop crochet in the colors shown here. Or, make it in the traditional manner using white or ecru crochet cotton.

The 60x80-inch oval cloth is worked in rounds of lacy shell, picot, and cluster stitches and features a beautiful floral-motif border. The exquisite stitch patterns actually are easy to master because they are all based on the basic crochet stitches—chain, single, and double crochet.

# ELEGANT HEIRLOOMS FOR YOUR HOME

Few needlework patterns are as enduringly popular as pineapple crochet. A traditional symbol of warm hospitality, the pineapple pattern is a favorite choice for tablecloth and doily designs or any item that might be used for special occasions or elegant entertaining.

The beautifully detailed tablecloth, *right*, is a stunning example of the pineapple crochet style. Oversize pineapple motifs are crocheted in rounds and fall from the table in graceful folds. The unusual center is stitched with large shells and chains to create a pinwheel effect that is a bold geometric contrast to the delicate lace that surrounds it.

This crocheted cloth is stitched with heavy-weight crochet cotton and measures 72 inches in diameter. It also would make a stunning centerpiece doily for a large round table if it were worked with a finer thread and a smaller hook. Whatever size you decide to stitch, you'll find that this appealing pattern is equally appropriate for both Victorian and country decor.

The exquisite knitted coverlet, *opposite*, is an old and treasured pattern. Wonderfully textured and delicately stitched, this versatile old-time pattern is a knitter's dream. Although it was designed as a coverlet for a twin-size bed, the pattern is easily adapted to make a larger size bedspread as well as other lovely home accessories.

For example, you may wish to stitch a few shorter versions of the textured panels to make place mats or a table runner. Or, consider how pretty the leaf-patterned panels would look as inserts for ready-to-finish shutters. However you decide to interpret this antique design, you'll find it adds an heirloom touch to any room.

The bed throw shown consists of classic leaf-pattern and diagonal stockinette-stitch panels. Panels are knitted individually and stitched together. An unusual knitted edging trims the border.

When complete, the coverlet is 63x86 inches. The twin-size coverlet is made with fifteen panels. For a larger bed, simply stitch a few more panels. To make the coverlet longer, knit additional inches onto each of the panels.

Delicate cotton thread and Size 0 knitting needles were used to make this bed throw. But if you are looking for a project that is a little less time-consuming, this antique design would make an equally lovely afghan using worsted-weight or sport yarn and needles several sizes larger.

# ELEGANT HEIRLOOMS

Crocheting a bedspread is, admittedly, a challenge. But the results are well worth the effort. For not only are you making a lovely bedspread that you will enjoy for a lifetime, you're also creating a precious heirloom—one that will be treasured by generations to come.

Timeless quality and enduring charm are two of the beautiful features of the crocheted bedcover shown here. Another appealing aspect is that it's worked in easy-to-carry pieces. So, you can take it along and work on it anytime, anywhere.

The pattern is a classic. Crocheted in rounds, the hexagon motifs feature a ring of pineapples worked in popcorn stitch. Simple chain and double-crochet stitches create the mesh that completes each motif. When the motifs are stitched together, dainty medallions are formed at the joinings. Knotted fringe around three sides enhances the gracefully shaped edges of the design.

Because the motifs are stitched individually and then joined together, you can make this traditional spread to fit any size bed. Each motif measures about 7 inches from side to side and 8 inches from point to point diagonally.

For a twin-size bedspread, approximately 72x108 inches in size, you'll need 202 motifs. For a 96x108-inch double-size spread, make 283 motifs. A 108-inch-square queen-to-king-size spread is composed of 337 motifs.

For a quick-stitch version of this nostalgic piece of needlework, you might try making the motifs in a heavier weight cotton thread or even sport yarn.

Or stitch several of the motifs atop an oversize occasional pillow. Backed with a pretty print or a pastel fabric, it will add a touch of romance to any room.

## Five O'Clock Tea Crocheted Cloth

Shown on pages 86–87.
Finished size is approximately 50 inches square. Edging at the widest point is 8 inches.

**MATERIALS**

J & P Coats "Big Ball" crochet cotton, Size 30 (400-yard balls): 7 balls

1⅛ yards of 38-inch-wide linen or other fabric for a 34¼-inch square cloth before edging

Size 12 steel crochet hook

**Abbreviations:** Page 211.

**Gauge:** 8 sps or bls = 1 inch; 6 rows = 1 inch.

**INSTRUCTIONS**

Ch 137. *Row 1* (right side): **Dc in eighth ch from hook—beg sp made; ch 2, sk 2 ch, dc in next ch—sp made; dc in next 6 ch—2 blocks (bls) made; ch 2, sk 2 ch, sc in next ch, ch 2, sk 2 ch, dc in next ch—V-bl made; dc in 6 ch—2 bls made;** (ch 2, sk 2 ch, dc in next ch) 28 times; work 2 bls over next 6 ch; work V-bl over next 6 ch, 2 bls over next 6 ch, 2 sps over last 6 ch. Ch 5, turn.

*Row 2:* **Sk first dc, dc in next dc—beg sp over sp made; ch 2, dc in next dc—sp over sp made; dc in next 6 dc—2 bls over 2 bls made; ch 5, sk V-bl, dc in next dc—2 bl-sps over V-bl made;** make 2 bls over 2 bls; make 28 sps; work 2 bls over 2 bls; work 2 bl-sp over V-bl; work 2 bls over 2 bls; work 2 sps over 2 sps; ch 10, turn.

*Row 3:* **Dc in eighth ch from hook, ch 2, sk 2 ch, dc in next dc—2 sps inc at beg of row; (2 dc in next ch-2 sp, dc in next dc) twice—2 bls over 2 bl-sps made; ch 2, sk 2 dc, sc in next dc, ch 2, sk 2 dc, dc in next dc—V-bl over 2 bls made;** work 5 dc in next ch-5 lp, dc in next dc—2 bls over 2 bl-sps made; make 19 sps; make 1 bl over sp; make 10 sps; V-bl over 2 bls; 2 bls over 2 bl-sps; V-bl over 2 bls; 2 sps over 2 sps; ch 5, turn.

Beg with Row 4 of Chart I, *below*, inc and dec as indicated through Row 76. *Note:* To inc at end of row, ch 10, turn; dc in eighth ch from hook, ch 2, dc in next dc. To dec at end of row, do not work over rem sts of row; to dec at beg of row, sl st across required number of stitches to the starting point to begin the next row; ch-5 to count as dc and ch-2 of beg sp or ch 3 to count as first dc when beg of row begins with bl (Rows 30, 32, and 34).

Beg with Row 77, work entire first point through Row 86 of Chart I; then join thread at point marked by arrow on Row 77 and complete second point. Fasten off.

**5 O'CLOCK TEA CLOTH**
**CHART 1/ CORNER**

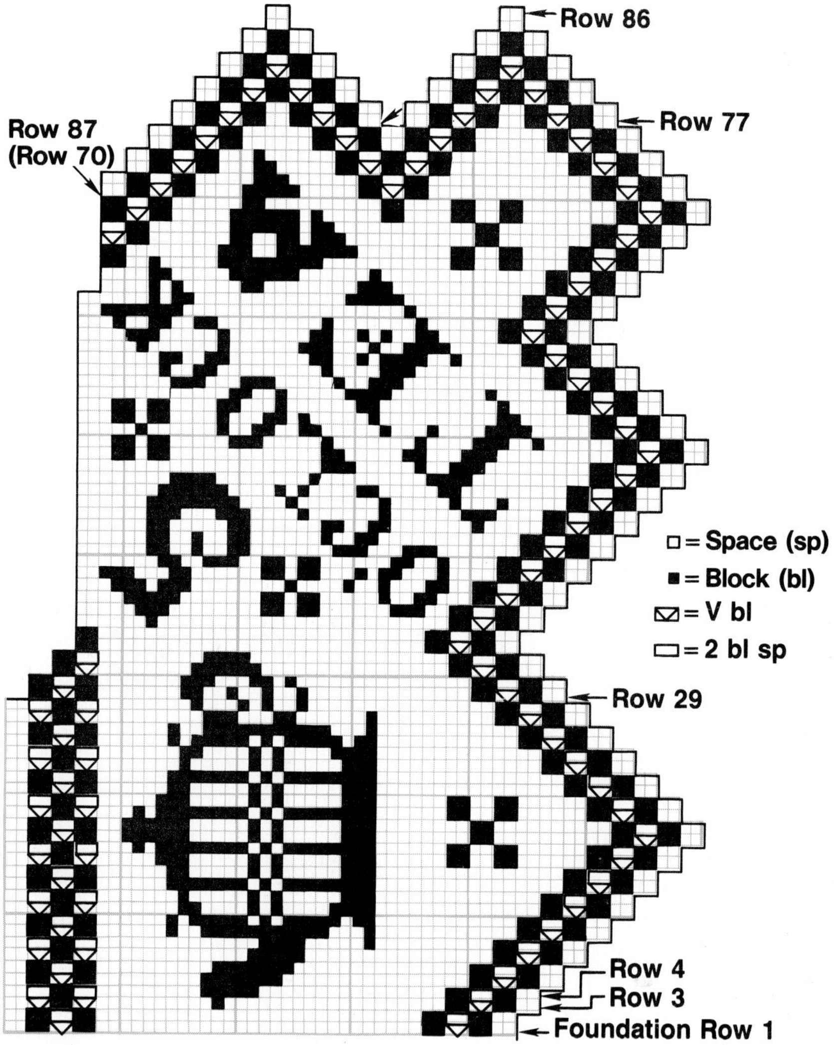

Turn corner by joining thread, with right side facing, at arrow at beg of Row 70 of Chart I and work across end of Rows 70 through 29 as follows (and as indicated on Chart II, *right*).

*Row 87:* Ch 5, dc in top of dc of next row (Row 69)—beg sp made. Ch 2, dc in third ch of next row (Row 68)—sp made. 2 dc in end of same row; dc in top of dc of next row (Row 67). 2 dc in end of same row, dc in third ch of next row (Row 66)—2 bls made. Ch 2 and sc in top of dc of next row (Row 65). Ch 2 and dc in third ch of following row (Row 64)—V-bl made. 2 dc in end of same row, dc in top of dc of next row (Row 63). 2 dc in end of same row then join with sl st in dc of next sp of next row (Row 62) to complete bl. Sl st across adjacent top edge of end sp of same row (Row 62). Turn to beg next row.

Continue following Chart II for Rows 88–94 across ends of rows of Chart I and joining to rows of Chart I with sl st. Then sl st across tops of sps or bl at end of rows of Chart I to reach height to begin next row instead of working a turning-ch.

Follow Chart II from A through B once. Rep from A through C once. Then beg with Row 3 of Chart I, rep through Row 86 to work next corner. Continue in this way until 4 corners have been made, working last side from Rows 87 to 94, then from A through B once, then from A through D once. Fasten off. Sew first and last row together.

FINISHING: Center edging over fabric, mark fabric along 4 sides of edging. Remove edging. Allowing ⅛ inch for edging to overlap fabric, mark fold line for hem, then mark cutting line on fabric, allowing for 1¾-inch hem, plus ¼ inch to turn under cut edge on each side; miter corners. Sew edging to fabric; center overlapping fabric over inner edge of edging.

**5 O'CLOCK TEA CLOTH**
**CHART 2/ SIDE EDGE**

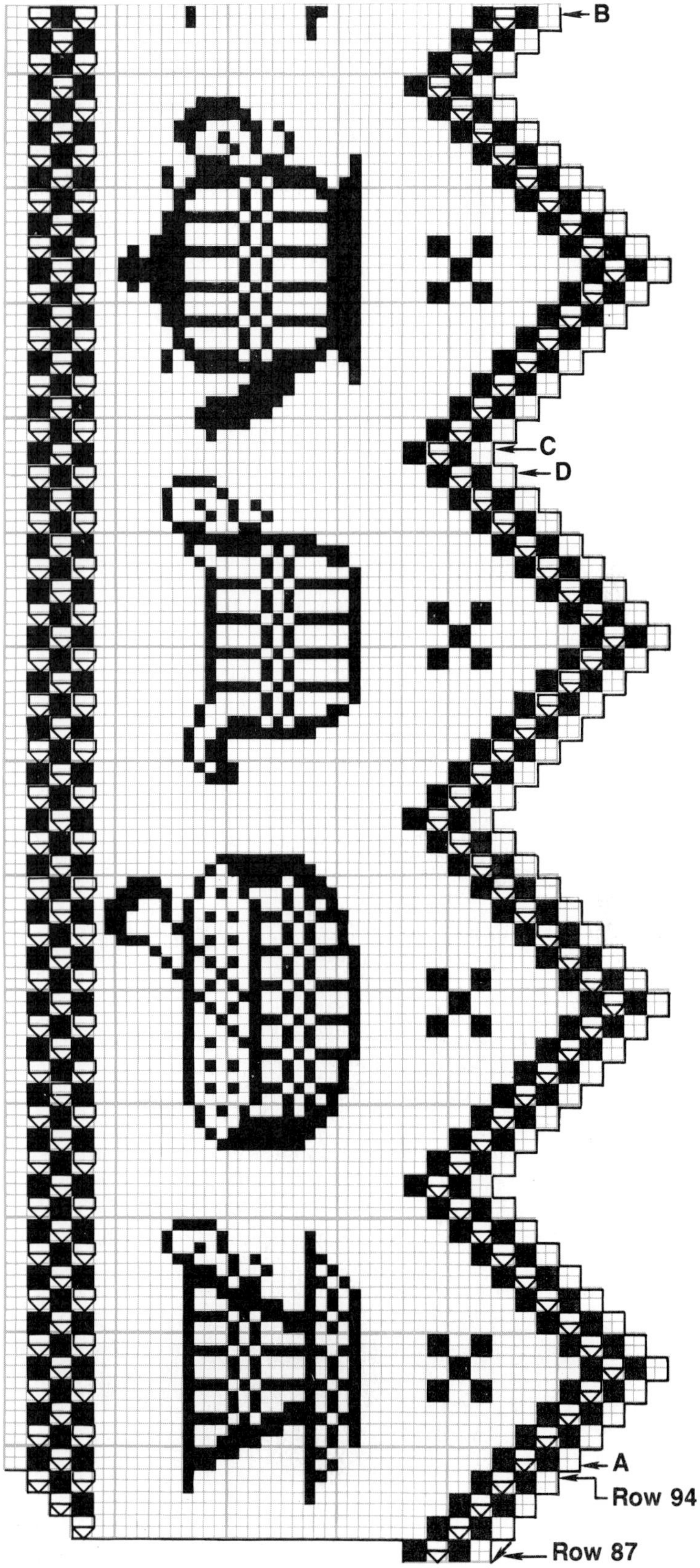

## Crocheted Oval Tablecloth

Shown on pages 88–89.
Finished size is approximately 60x80 inches. (This cloth also may be stitched in a single color; adjust amounts of thread accordingly.)

**MATERIALS**

American Thread "Puritan" mercerized crochet cotton (250-yard balls): 17 balls of No. 203 ecru, 5 balls of No. 226 shaded pinks, 1 ball of No. 223 shaded yellows, 4 balls of No. 221 shaded greens

Size 7 steel crochet hook

**Abbreviations:** Page 211.

**INSTRUCTIONS**

*Rnd 1:* With ecru, * **ch 5, sl st in fifth ch from hook—ch-5 picot made,** rep from * twice, sl st in base of first picot (one end made), ** ch 3, hdc in third st from hook, make ch-5 picot, rep from ** 30 times, work 2 more ch-5 picots, sl st in base of third picot from hook (other end made), * ch 3, hdc in third st from hook, sl st in base of opposite hdc, make ch-5 picot, sl st in base of opposite picot, rep from last * 29 times; ch 3, hdc in third st from hook, join with sl st in base of first picot.

*Rnd 2:* Sl st to center of next picot, ch 3, dc in same space, * ch 5, 2 dc in next ch-5 picot, rep from * around, ending ch 2, dc in top of ch-3 (this brings thread in position for next rnd).

*Rnd 3:* Sc in same space, ch 5, sc in same lp, (ch 5, sc in next lp, ch 5, sc in same lp) 3 times; * ch 5, sc in next lp, rep from * 29 times, ch 5, sc in same lp, (ch 5, sc in next lp, ch 5, sc in same lp) 3 times; complete rnd to correspond, ending ch 2, dc in first sc at beg of rnd.

*Rnd 4:* Ch 3, dc in same lp, * ch 5, 2 dc in next lp, rep from * around, ending ch 2, dc in top of ch-3 at beg of rnd.

*Rnd 5:* Sc in same space, (ch 5, sc in next lp, ch 5, sc in same lp) 8 times; * ch 5, sc in next lp, rep from * 29 times; (ch 5, sc in same lp, ch 5, sc in next lp) 8 times; complete rnd in ch-5 lps, end ch 2, dc in first sc.

*Rnd 6:* Same as Rnd 4.

*Rnd 7:* Sc in same space, * ch 5, sc in next lp, rep from * around, ending ch 2, dc in first sc. Fasten off ecru.

*Rnd 8:* Join shaded green in last loop made, and work same as Rnd 4. Fasten off.

*Rnd 9* (motif): With shaded yellows, ** ch 5, join with sl st to form ring; ch 3, **(yo, draw up lp in ring, yo, draw through 2 lps on hook) 4 times; yo draw through all lps on hook—cluster (cl) made.** Ch 3, drop lp from hook, insert hook in third st to right of any dc of Rnd 8, pull dropped lp through, ch 3, drop lp from hook, insert hook to left of same dc group in third st of next lp of Rnd 8, pull dropped lp through, ch 3, work cl in ring, * ch 9, cl in ring, rep from * once; ch 9, join to first cl. Fasten off.

Rep motifs from ** in Rnd 9 all around, joining motif to previous motif in center of lp and to Rnd 8 of the cloth same as last motif. Then join the final motif to first motif made in the corresponding lp on the side of the first motif. Fasten off.

*Rnd 10:* Join green thread in third ch of any free lp of any motif, * **(ch 7, sl st in fifth st from hook for picot—ch-7 picot made) twice,** ch 2, sk 3 sts of ch, sc in next ch of same lp, (work ch-7 picot) twice, ch 2, sc in third st of next lp, rep from * around, join to first ch of beg ch-7 lp. Fasten off.

*Rnd 11:* Join ecru bet next 2 picots, ch 3, 2 dc in same space, * ch 5, 3 dc bet picots of next lp, rep from * around, ending ch 2, dc in top of ch-3.

*Rnd 12:* * (Work ch-7 picot) twice, ch 2, sc in next lp, rep from * around, join in top of ch-3.

*Rnd 13* (inc round): Work same as Rnd 11 working inc in 9 lps at each end as follows: * 2 dc, ch 5, 2 dc bet next 2 picots, ch 5, rep from * 8 times, complete rnd—36 even lps bet inc lps on sides.

*Rnds 14–21:* Rep Rnds 12 and 11 alternately.

*Rnd 22:* Rep Rnd 12.

*Rnd 23:* Rep Rnd 13—45 even lps bet inc lps on each side.

*Rnds 24–26:* Rep Rnds 12, 11, and 12. Fasten off thread at end of Rnd 26.

*Rnd 27:* Join green bet next 2 picots and work as for Rnd 11. Fasten off.

*Rnd 28:* With shaded yellow, rep Rnd 9. Fasten off.

*Rnd 29:* Attach green in third st of any free lp of any motif, * **[work ch-7 picot, work ch-5 picot, sl st in base of first picot—double picot made; ch 9, sl st in fifth st from hook for picot—ch-9 picot made; work ch-5 picot, sl st in base of previous picot, ch 2—double picot loop made]**, sk 3 sts of ch of same lp of motif, sc in next st, rep between [ ]s to make another double picot loop; sk 2 lps bet motifs, sc in third st of next lp of next motif, rep from * around ending to correspond. Fasten off.

*Rnd 30:* Join ecru bet next 2 double picots, ch 3, 3 dc in same space, * ch 5, sk next 2 groups of picots, 4 dc in next lp bet 2 double picots, rep from * around, join in top of ch-3.

*Rnd 31:* Sl st to center of next lp, * work double picot loop (same as in Rnd 29), sc in next lp, rep from * around ending to correspond, join.

*Rnds 32–33:* Rep Rnds 30–31.

*Rnd 34:* Sl st bet next 2 double picots, ch 3, 4 dc in same lp, * ch 6, sk next 2 groups of picots, 5 dc in lp bet next 2 double picots, rep from * around, join in top of ch-3.

*Rnd 35:* Sl st to center of next lp, * work a double picot loop working *ch-8* in lieu of ch-7 at beg of loop and a *ch-3* in lieu of a ch-2 at end of lp, sc in next lp, rep from * around, join.

*Rnds 36–37:* Rep Rnds 34–35.

*Rnd 38:* Same as Rnd 34, except work 6 dc bet picots and make ch-7 lps in lieu of ch-6 lps.

*Rnd 39:* Work same as Rnd 35 working *ch-9* in lieu of ch-8 at beg of loop and *ch-4* in lieu of ch-3, join.

*Rnds 40–49:* Rep Rnds 38 and 39 alternately.

*Rnd 50:* Sl st to picot, sc in same space, 9 dc in lp bet picots, sc on other side of picots, * ch 5, sc before next picots, 9 dc bet picots, sc on other side of picots, rep from * around, ending to correspond, join in first sc. Fasten off.

*Rnd 51:* Join green in next dc, **ch 4 (counts as 1 trc), trc in each of next 3 dc, 3 trc in next dc, trc in each of next 4 dc—shell made,** sc in next lp, * trc in each of the next 4 dc, 3 trc in next dc, trc in each of next 4 dc, sc in next lp, rep from * around. Join to top of ch-4. Fasten off.

*Rnd 52* (motif): With pink, ch 5, join to form ring, cl in ring, ch 3, drop lp from hook, insert hook in fourth trc to right of any shell of Rnd 51, pull dropped lp through, ch 3, drop lp, sk 3 trc of same shell, insert hook in next trc, pull lp through, ch 3, (cl in ring, ch 9) 3 times, join to top of first cl. Fasten off.

Work a second motif and join to previous motif as follows: Cl in ring, ch 3, sl st in third ch on side of first motif, ch 3, sk 3 ch of first motif, sl st in next ch, ch 3, cl in ring, ch 3, sl st in fourth trc of next shell, ch 3, sk 3 trc of same shell, sl st in next trc, ch 3, cl in ring, ch 9, cl in ring, ch 9, join to top of first cl. Rep second motif around, joining last motif to first motif to correspond. Fasten off.

*Rnd 53:* With green, ch 5, join to form ring, cl in ring, ch 9, cl in ring, ch 3, drop lp from hook, insert hook in third st of free ch-9 lp to right of joining of any 2 motifs, draw dropped lp through, ch 8, sl st in third st of next ch-9 lp to left of joining of same 2 motifs, ch 3, cl in same ring, ch 9, cl in same ring, ch 13, join to top of first cl. Fasten off.

Rep last motif around, joining to Rnd 52 in same manner and joining at side of ch-9 lps in same manner as last motif rnd.

*Rnd 54:* With ecru, ch 5, join to form ring, cl in ring, ch 12, cl in ring, ch 13, drop lp from hook, insert hook in third st of ch-13 lp to right of joining of any 2 motifs, draw dropped lp through, ch 7, drop lp, insert hook in third st of next ch-13 lp to left of same joining of same 2 motifs, draw dropped lp through, ch 3, cl in ring, ch 12, cl in ring, ch 13, join to top of first cl. Fasten off.

Work a second motif, joining to previous motif as follows: Cl in ring, ch 4, sl st to fourth ch on side of first motif, ch 4, sk 4 ch of first motif, sl st in next ch, ch 4, cl in ring, ch 13, complete motifs and joining same as previous motif. Fasten off.

*Rnd 55:* Attach ecru in any joining bet motifs, sc in same space, * 11 dc in next ch-13 lp, sc bet joinings, rep from * around, join to first sc. Fasten off.

*Rnd 56:* Join green in same sp as join, ch 1, sc in same sp, * hdc in next dc, dc in each of next 2 dc, trc in each of next 2 dc, 3 trc in next dc, trc in each of next 2 dc, dc in each of next 2 dc, hdc in next dc, sc in next sc, rep from * around, join to first sc. Fasten off.

*Rnd 57:* Join ecru in center trc of any shell grp, * ch 4, 2 dc in fourth ch from hook, (work ch-5 picot, ch 4, 2 dc in fourth ch from hook) three times, sc in center trc of next shell grp, rep from * around, ending to correspond, join to first ch of beg ch-4. Fasten off.

*Rnd 58:* Join ecru in center of ch-5 picot, ch 3, 6 dc in same space, * ch 4, 2 dc in fourth ch from hook, work a ch-5 picot, ch 4, 2 dc in fourth ch from hook, 7 dc in center of next picot, rep from * around, join to top of ch-3. Fasten off.

*Rnds 59–60:* Rep Rnd 58.

*Rnd 61:* Sl st to next picot (or fasten off at end of Rnd 60 and join thread in ch-5 picot), * ch 4, 2 dc in fourth ch from hook, (work ch-5 picot, ch 4, 2 dc in fourth ch from hook) three times, sc in next picot, rep from * around, ending to correspond, join.

*Rnd 62:* Sl st to center picot, ch 3, in same sp work dc, 5 trc, 2 dc, * ch 5, 2 trc in fifth ch from hook, work ch-5 picot, ch 5, 2 trc in fifth ch from hook, in center of ch-5 picot work 2 dc, 5 trc, 2 dc, rep from * around, ending to correspond, join.

*Rnd 63:* Rep Rnd 62. Fasten off.

*Rnd 64:* Join green in ch-5 picot and rep Rnd 62. Fasten off.

*Rnd 65:* Join pink in ch-5 picot, * ch 5, 2 trc in fifth ch from hook, work ch-5 picot, ch 5, 2 trc in fifth ch from hook, ch 7, join with sl st to seventh ch from hook to form ring, sl st in ring, ch 5, **[yo hook twice, draw up loop in ring, (yo, draw through 2 lps on hook) twice]; rep bet [ ]s 2 more times—3-trc cl made, (ch 5, rep bet [ ]s 3 times—4 trc cl made) twice.** Ch 5, 3-trc cl in ring, ch 5, sl st in ring, ch 5, 2 trc in fifth ch from hook, work ch-5 picot, ch 5, 2 trc in fifth ch from hook, sc in next picot, rep from * around, join.

*Rnd 66:* Sl st to next picot, ch 5, sc in top of next cl, * (work ch-7 picot, work a ch-5 picot, sl st in base of first picot, ch 2, sc in next lp, work ch-7 picot, work a ch-5 picot, sl st in base of first picot, ch 2, sc in top of next cl) three times, ch 5, sc in next picot, ch 4, sc in next picot, ch 5, sc in top of next cluster st, rep from * around, join, cut thread.

FINISHING: Pin and stretch to measure 60x80 inches. (If necessary divide into quarter sections and block one section at a time.)

# Pineapple Tablecloth

Shown on page 90.
The finished cloth is 72 inches in diameter.

**MATERIALS**
Coats and Clark Red Heart Luster Sheen Knit and Crochet Yarn (2-ounce skeins): 17 skeins of No. 805 natural
Size E aluminum crochet hook

**Abbreviations:** Page 211.

**INSTRUCTIONS**
Beg at center, ch 8; join with sl st to form ring.

*Rnd 1:* Ch 3, 19 dc in ring; join with sl st to top of beg ch-3.

*Rnd 2:* Ch 3, dc in same place as sl st, 2 dc in each dc around; join to top of ch-3.

*Rnd 3:* (Ch 10, sk 3 dc, sc in next dc) 9 times; ch 10, sk 3 dc, join with sl st to first ch of beg ch-10.

*Rnd 4:* In *each* ch-10 lp around work (3 sc, 2 hdc, 5 dc, ch 10, 5 dc, 2 hdc, 3 sc); join with sl st to sc at beg of rnd.

*Rnd 5:* Sl st in each of next 9 sts and into ch-10 lp; ch 3, in same lp make (9 dc, ch 10, 10 dc); * in next lp make (10 dc, ch 10, 10 dc); rep from * around; join with sl st to top of ch-3 at beg of rnd.

*Rnd 6:* Sl st in each of next 9 sts and into ch-10 lp; ch 4, in same lp make (9 trc, ch 10, 10 trc); * in next ch-10 lp make (10 trc, ch 10, 10 trc); rep from * around; join with sl st to top of ch-4.

*Rnd 7:* Sl st up to ch-10 lp; ch 4, in same lp make (9 trc, ch 10, 10 trc); * ch 5, in next ch-10 lp make (10 trc, ch 10, 10 trc); rep from * around; end ch 5, join with sl st to top of beg ch-4.

*Rnd 8:* Sl st up to ch-10 lp; ch 4, in same lp make (9 trc, ch 10, 10 trc); * ch 13, sl st in eighth ch from hook, ch 5, in next ch-10 lp, make (10 trc, ch 10, 10 trc); rep from * around, ending with ch 5, dtr (yo 3 times) in top of beg ch-4; ch 8, *turn,* sl st in eighth ch from hook.

*Rnd 9: Turn;* with right side facing, sl st into ch-8 lp just made; ch 3, in same lp make 2 dc, ch 2, 3 dc; * ch 5, in next ch-10 lp make (10 trc, ch 10, 10 trc); ch 5, sk next ch-5 lp; in next ch-8 lp make **3 dc, ch 2, 3 dc—shell made**; rep from * around omitting last shell in pat rep; join last ch-5 with sl st to top of beg ch-3.

*Rnd 10:* Sl st in next 2 dc and into ch-2 sp, **ch 3, in same ch-2 sp make 2 dc, ch 2, 3 dc—beg shell in shell made.** * Ch 7, 20 trc in next ch-10 lp, ch 7, **make (3 dc, ch 2, 3 dc) in next ch-2 sp—shell in shell made**; rep from * around omitting last shell in pat rep; join last ch-7 to top of beg ch-3.

*Note:* Unless otherwise indicated, all rnds beg with sl st into next 2 dc and into ch-2 sp.

*Rnd 11:* Make beg shell in shell, * ch 5, trc in first trc, (ch 1, trc in next trc) 19 times; ch 5, shell in shell. Rep from * around omitting last shell in pat rep; join last ch-5 with sl st to top of beg ch-3.

*Rnd 12:* Make beg shell in shell, * ch 5, sc in first ch-1 sp, (ch 3, sc in next ch-1 sp) 18 times; ch 5, shell in shell; rep from * around omitting last shell in pat rep; join last ch-5 with sl st to top of ch-3—18 lps.

*Rnd 13:* Make beg shell in shell, * ch 5, sc in first ch-3 lp, (ch 3, sc in next lp) 17 times, ch 5; shell in shell; rep from * around omitting shell in last pat rep; join last ch-5 with sl st to top of beg ch-3—17 lps.

*Note:* Unless stated otherwise, omit last shell in last pattern rep in all rnds that follow, and end as cited.

*Rnd 14:* Make beg shell in shell, * ch 5, sc in first ch-3 lp, (ch 3, sc in next lp) 16 times, ch 5, shell in shell; rep from * around; join last ch-5 with sl st to top of beg ch-3—16 pineapple lps.

*Rnd 15:* Make beg shell in shell, * ch 5, sc in first ch-3 lp, (ch 3, sc in next lp) 15 times, ch 5, shell in shell; rep from * around; join last ch-5 with sl st to top of ch-3—15 pineapple lps.

*Rnd 16:* Make beg shell in shell, * ch 5, sc in first ch-3 lp, (ch 3, sc in next lp) 14 times, ch 5, shell in shell; rep from * around; join last ch-5 with sl st to top of ch-3—14 pineapple lps.

*Rnd 17:* Beg shell in shell, * ch 5, sc in first ch-3 lp, (ch 3, sc in next lp) 13 times, ch 5, shell in shell; rep from * around; join last ch-5 with sl st to top of beg ch-3—13 pineapple loops.

*Rnd 18:* Sl st to ch-2 sp, ch 3, make (2 dc, ch 2, 3 dc, ch 2, 3 dc) in same sp. * Ch 5, sc in first ch-3 lp, (ch 3, sc in next lp) 12 times, ch 5; (3 dc, ch 2, 3 dc, ch 2, 3 dc) in next ch-2 sp; rep from * around; join last ch-5 to top of beg ch-3—12 lps.

*Rnd 19:* Beg shell in first ch-2 sp, shell in next ch-2 sp, * ch 5; sc in first ch-3 lp, (ch 3, sc in next lp) 11 times, ch 5; shell in *each* of next two ch-2 sps; rep from * around; join last ch-5 with sl st to top of beg ch-3—11 pineapple loops.

*Rnd 20:* Beg shell in shell, * ch 5, shell in next shell, ch 5, sc in first ch-3 lp, (ch 3, sc in next lp) 10 times, ch 5; shell in next shell; rep from * around; join last ch-5 with sl st to top of beg ch-3—10 pineapple loops.

*Rnd 21:* Beg shell in shell, * ch 7, shell in next shell, ch 5, sc in first ch-3 lp, (ch 3, sc in next lp) 9 times, ch 5; shell in next shell; rep from * around; join last ch-5 with sl st to top of beg ch-3—9 pineapple loops.

*Rnd 22:* Beg shell in shell, * ch 5, sc over the 2 ch-lps of 2 previous rnds, ch 5, shell in shell, ch 5, sc in first ch-3 lp, (ch 3, sc in next lp) 8 times, ch 5; shell in next shell; rep from * around; join last ch-5 with sl st to top of beg ch-3—8 loops.

*Rnd 23:* Beg shell in shell, * ch 7, sc in sc, ch 7, shell in next shell, ch

5, sc in first ch-3 lp, (ch 3, sc in next lp) 7 times, ch 5; shell in next shell. Rep from * around; join last ch-5 with sl st to top of beg ch-3—7 pineapple loops.

*Rnd 24:* Beg shell in shell, * ch 5, make (dtr, ch 10, dtr) in next sc, ch 5, shell in shell, ch 5, sc in first ch-3 lp, (ch 3, sc in next lp) 6 times, ch 5; shell in shell; rep from * around; join last ch-5 with sl st to top of beg ch-3—6 pineapple loops.

*Rnd 25:* Beg shell in shell, * ch 5, 20 trc in ch-10 lp, ch 5, shell in shell, ch 5, sc in first ch-3 lp, (ch 3, sc in next lp) 5 times, ch 5, shell in shell; rep from * around; join last ch-5 with sl st to top of beg ch-3—5 pineapple loops.

*Rnd 26:* Beg shell in shell, * ch 5, 2 trc in first trc, trc in each of next 6 sts, 2 trc in next st, trc in next 4 sts, 2 trc in next st, trc in next 6 sts, 2 trc in last st—24 trc; ch 5, shell in shell, ch 5, sc in first ch-3 lp, (ch 3, sc in next lp) 4 times, ch 5; shell in shell; rep from * around; join last ch-5 with sl st to top of beg ch-3—4 pineapple loops.

*Rnd 27:* Beg shell in shell, * ch 5, trc in first trc, (ch 1, trc in next trc) 23 times; ch 5, shell in shell, ch 5, sc in first ch-3 lp, (ch 3, sc in next lp) 3 times, ch 5, shell in shell; rep from * around; join last ch-5 with sl st to top of beg ch-3—3 pineapple loops.

*Rnd 28:* Beg shell in shell, * ch 5, sc in first ch-1 lp, (ch 3, sc in next lp) 22 times; ch 5, shell in shell, ch 5, sc in first ch-3 lp, (ch 3, sc in next lp) twice, ch 5, shell in shell; rep from * around; join last ch-5 with sl st to top of beg ch-3—22 (2) pineapple loops.

*Rnd 29:* Beg shell in shell, * ch 5, sc in first ch-3 lp, (ch 3, sc in next lp) 21 times; ch 5, shell in shell, ch 5, sc in first ch-3 lp, ch 3, sc in next lp, ch 5, shell in shell; rep from * around; join last ch-5 to top of beg ch-3—21 (1) pineapple loops.

*Rnd 30:* Beg shell in shell, * ch 5, sc in first ch-3 lp, (ch 3, sc in next lp) 20 times; ch 5, shell in shell, ch 5, sc in ch-3 lp, ch 5, shell in shell. Rep from * around; join last ch-5 to top of beg ch-3—20 pineapple lps.

*Rnd 31:* Beg shell in shell, * ch 5, sc in first ch-3 lp, (ch 3, sc in next lp) 19 times; ch 5, shell in shell, ch 5, sc in sc, ch 5; shell in shell; rep from * around; join last ch-5 to top of beg ch-3—19 pineapple loops.

*Rnd 32:* Beg shell in shell, * ch 5, sc in first ch-3 lp, (ch 3, sc in next lp) 18 times, ch 5, shell in shell; sk next 2 ch-5 lps, shell in next shell. Rep from * around, ending sk 2 ch-5 lps, join with sl st to top of beg ch-3—18 pineapple loops.

*Rnd 33:* Beg shell in shell, * ch 5, sc in first ch-3 lp, (ch 3, sc in next lp) 17 times, ch 5, shell in shell, ch 5; shell in next shell; rep from * around; join last ch-5 with sl st to top of beg ch-3—17 pineapple loops.

*Rnd 34:* Beg shell in shell, * ch 5, sc in first ch-3 lp, (ch 3, sc in next lp) 16 times, ch 5, shell in shell, ch 7; shell in next shell; rep from * around; join last ch-7 to top of beg ch-3—16 pineapple loops.

*Rnd 35:* Beg shell in shell, * ch 5, sc in first ch-3 lp, (ch 3, sc in next lp) 15 times, ch 5, shell in shell, ch 5, sc over 2 ch-lps of 2 previous rnds, ch 5, shell in shell; rep from * around; join last ch-5 to top of beg ch-3—15 pineapple loops.

*Rnd 36:* Beg shell in shell, * ch 5, sc in first ch-3 lp, (ch 3, sc in next lp) 14 times, ch 5, shell in shell, ch 7, sc in sc, ch 7, shell in shell; rep from * around; join last ch-7 to top of beg ch-3—14 pineapple loops.

*Rnd 37:* Beg shell in shell, * ch 5, sc in first ch-3 lp, (ch 3, sc in next lp) 13 times, ch 5, shell in shell, ch 11, sc in sc, ch 11, shell in shell. Rep from * around; join last ch-11 to top of beg ch-3—13 pineapple loops.

*Rnd 38:* Beg shell in shell, * ch 5, sc in first ch-3 lp, (ch 3, sc in next lp) 12 times, ch 5, shell in shell, ch 5, dtr in ch-11 lp, ch 12, dtr in next ch-11 lp, ch 5, shell in shell; rep from * around; join last ch-5 to top of beg ch-3—12 pineapple loops.

*Rnd 39:* Beg shell in shell, * ch 5, sc in first ch-3 lp, (ch 3, sc in next lp) 11 times, ch 5, shell in shell, ch 5, 22 trc in ch-12 lp, ch 5, shell in shell; rep from * around; join last ch-5 top of beg ch-3—11 pineapple loops.

*Rnd 40:* Beg shell in shell, * ch 5, sc in first ch-3 lp, (ch 3, sc in next lp) 10 times, ch 5, shell in shell, ch 5, (2 trc in next trc, trc in each of next 2 trc) 7 times, 2 trc in last trc—30 trc; ch 5; shell in shell; rep from * around; join last ch-5 to top of beg ch-3—10 pineapple loops.

*Rnd 41:* Beg shell in shell, * ch 5, sc in first ch-3 lp, (ch 3, sc in next lp) 9 times, ch 5, shell in shell, ch 5, 2 trc in first trc, trc in next 9 trc, 2 trc in next trc, trc in next 8 trc, 2 trc in next trc, trc in next 9 trc, 2 trc in last trc—34 trc; ch 5, shell in shell. Rep from * around; join last ch-5 to top of beg ch-3—9 pineapple loops.

*Rnd 42:* Beg shell in shell, * ch 5, sc in first ch-3 lp, (ch 3, sc in next lp) 8 times, ch 5, shell in shell, ch 5, trc in first trc, (ch 1, trc in next trc) 33 times; ch 5, shell in shell; rep from * around; join last ch-5 to top of beg ch-3—8 pineapple loops.

*Rnd 43:* Beg shell in shell, * ch 5, sc in first ch-3 lp, (ch 3, sc in next lp) 7 times, ch 5, shell in shell, ch 5, sc in first ch-1 sp, (ch 3, sc in next ch-1 sp) 32 times; ch 5, shell in shell; rep from * around; join last ch-5 to top of beg ch-3—7 (32) pineapple loops.

*Rnd 44:* Beg shell in shell, * ch 5, sc in first ch-3 lp, (ch 3, sc in next lp) 6 times, ch 5, shell in shell, ch 5, sc in first ch-3 lp, (ch 3, sc in next lp) 31 times; ch 5, shell in shell; rep from * around, join last ch-5 to top of beg ch-3—6 (31) pineapple loops.

*Rnd 45:* Beg shell in shell, * ch 5, sc in first ch-3 lp, (ch 3, sc in next lp) 5 times, ch 5, shell in shell, ch 5, sc in first ch-3 lp, (ch 3, sc in next lp) 30 times; ch 5, shell in shell; rep from * around, join last ch-5 to top of beg ch-3—5 (30) pineapple loops.

*Rnd 46:* Beg shell in shell, * ch 6, sc in first ch-3 lp, (ch 3, sc in next lp) 4 times, ch 6, shell in shell, ch 6, sc in first ch-3 lp, (ch 3, sc in next lp) 29 times; ch 6, shell in shell; rep from * around; join last ch-6 to top of beg ch-3—4 (29) pineapple loops.

*continued*

*Rnd 47:* Beg shell in shell, * ch 6, sc in first ch-3 lp, (ch 3, sc in next lp) 3 times, ch 6, shell in shell, ch 6, sc in first ch-3 lp, (ch 3, sc in next lp) 28 times; ch 6, shell in shell; rep from * around; join last ch-6 to top of beg ch-3—3 (28) pineapple loops.

*Rnd 48:* Beg shell in shell, * ch 7, sc in first ch-3 lp, (ch 3, sc in next lp) twice, ch 7, shell in shell, ch 6, sc in first ch-3 lp, (ch 3, sc in next lp) 27 times; ch 6, shell in shell; rep from * around; join last ch-6 to top of beg ch-3—2 (27) pineapple loops.

*Rnd 49:* Beg shell in shell, * ch 7, sc in first ch-3 lp, ch 3, sc in next lp, ch 7, shell in shell, ch 6, sc in first ch-3 lp, (ch 3, sc in next lp) 26 times; ch 6, shell in shell; rep from * around; join last ch-6 to top of beg ch-3—1 (26) pineapple loops.

*Rnd 50:* Beg shell in shell, * ch 8, sc in ch-3 lp, ch 8, shell in shell, ch 6, sc in first ch-3 lp, (ch 3, sc in next lp) 25 times; ch 6, shell in shell; rep from * around; join last ch-6 to top of beg ch-3—25 pineapple loops.

*Rnd 51:* Beg shell in shell, * ch 10, sc in sc, ch 10, shell in shell, ch 6, sc in first ch-3 lp, (ch 3, sc in next lp) 24 times; ch 6, shell in shell; rep from * around; join last ch-6 to top of beg ch-3—24 pineapple loops.

*Rnd 52:* Beg shell in shell, * ch 10, shell in next shell, ch 6, sc in first ch-3 lp, (ch 3, sc in next lp) 23 times; ch 6, shell in shell; rep from * around; join last ch-6 to top of beg ch-3—23 pineapple loops.

*Rnd 53:* Beg shell in shell, * ch 10, shell in next shell, ch 6, sc in first ch-3 lp, (ch 3, sc in next lp) 22 times; ch 6, shell in shell; rep from * around; join last ch-6 to top of beg ch-3—22 pineapple loops.

*Rnd 54:* Beg shell in shell, * ch 6, sc over both ch-10 lps of 2 previous rnds, ch 6, shell in shell, ch 6, sc in first ch-3 lp, (ch 3, sc in next lp) 21 times; ch 6, shell in shell; rep from * around; join last ch-6 to top of beg ch-3—21 pineapple loops.

*Rnd 55:* Beg shell in shell, * (ch 6, sc in next ch-6 lp) twice, ch 6, shell in shell, ch 6, sc in first ch-3 lp, (ch 3, sc in next lp) 20 times; ch 6, shell in shell; rep from * around; join last ch-6 to top of beg ch-3—20 pineapple loops.

*Rnd 56:* Beg shell in shell, * (ch 6, sc in next ch-6 lp) 3 times; ch 6, shell in shell, ch 6, sc in first ch-3 lp, (ch 3, sc in next lp) 19 times; ch 6, shell in shell; rep from * around; join last ch-6 to top of beg ch-3—19 pineapple loops.

*Rnd 57:* Beg shell in shell, * (ch 6, sc in next ch-6 lp) 4 times; ch 6, shell in shell, ch 6, sc in first ch-3 lp, (ch 3, sc in next lp) 18 times; ch 6, shell in shell; rep from * around; join last ch-6 to top of beg ch-3—18 pineapple loops.

*Rnd 58:* Beg shell in shell, * (ch 6, sc in next ch-6 lp) 5 times; ch 6, shell in shell, ch 6, sc in first ch-3 lp, (ch 3, sc in next lp) 17 times; ch 6, shell in shell; rep from * around; join last ch-6 to top of beg ch-3—17 pineapple loops.

*Rnd 59:* Beg shell in shell, * (ch 6, sc in next ch-6 lp) 6 times; ch 6, shell in shell, ch 6, sc in first ch-3 lp, (ch 3, sc in next lp) 16 times; ch 6, shell in shell; rep from * around; join last ch-6 to top of beg ch-3—16 pineapple loops.

*Rnd 60:* Beg shell in shell, * (ch 6, sc in next ch-6 lp) 7 times; ch 6, shell in shell, ch 6, sc in first ch-3 lp, (ch 3, sc in next lp) 15 times; ch 6, shell in shell; rep from * around; join last ch-6 to top of beg ch-3—15 pineapple loops.

*Rnd 61:* Beg shell in shell, * (ch 6, sc in next ch-6 lp) 8 times; ch 6, shell in shell, ch 6, sc in first ch-3 lp, (ch 3, sc in next lp) 14 times; ch 6, shell in shell; rep from * around; join last ch-6 to top of beg ch-3—14 pineapple loops.

*Rnd 62:* Beg shell in shell, * (ch 6, sc in next ch-6 lp) 9 times; ch 6, shell in shell, ch 6, sc in first ch-3 lp, (ch 3, sc in next lp) 13 times; ch 6, shell in shell; rep from * around; join last ch-6 to top of beg ch-3—13 pineapple loops.

*Rnd 63:* Beg shell in shell, * (ch 6, sc in next ch-6 lp) 10 times; ch 6, shell in shell, ch 6, sc in first ch-3 lp, (ch 3, sc in next lp) 12 times; ch 6, shell in shell; rep from * around; join last ch-6 to top of beg ch-3—12 pineapple loops.

*Rnd 64:* Beg shell in shell, * (ch 6, sc in next ch-6 lp) 11 times; ch 6, shell in shell, ch 6, sc in first ch-3 lp, (ch 3, sc in next lp) 11 times; ch 6, shell in shell; rep from * around; join last ch-6 to top of beg ch-3—11 pineapple loops.

*Rnd 65:* Beg shell in shell, * (ch 6, sc in next ch-6 lp) 12 times; ch 6, shell in shell, ch 6, sc in first ch-3 lp, (ch 3, sc in next lp) 10 times; ch 6, shell in shell; rep from * around; join last ch-6 to top of beg ch-3—10 pineapple loops.

*Rnd 66:* Beg shell in shell, * (ch 6, sc in next ch-6 lp) 13 times; ch 6, shell in shell, ch 6, sc in first ch-3 lp, (ch 3, sc in next lp) 9 times; ch 6, shell in shell; rep from * around; join last ch-6 to top of beg ch-3—9 pineapple loops.

*Rnd 67:* Beg shell in shell, * (ch 6, sc in next ch-6 lp) 14 times; ch 6, shell in shell, ch 6, sc in first ch-3 lp, (ch 3, sc in next lp) 8 times; ch 6, shell in shell; rep from * around; join last ch-6 to top of beg ch-3—8 pineapple loops.

*Rnd 68:* Beg shell in shell, * (ch 6, sc in next ch-6 lp) 15 times; ch 6, shell in shell, ch 6, sc in first ch-3 lp, (ch 3, sc in next lp) 7 times; ch 6, shell in shell; rep from * around; join last ch-6 to top of beg ch-3—7 pineapple loops.

*Rnd 69:* Beg shell in shell, * (ch 6, sc in next ch-6 lp) 16 times; ch 6, shell in shell, ch 6, sc in first ch-3 lp, (ch 3, sc in next lp) 6 times; ch 6, shell in shell; rep from * around; join last ch-6 to top of beg ch-3—6 pineapple loops.

*Rnd 70:* Beg shell in shell, * (ch 6, sc in next ch-6 lp) 17 times; ch 6, shell in shell, ch 6, sc in first ch-3 lp, (ch 3, sc in next lp) 5 times; ch 6, shell in shell; rep from * around; join last ch-6 to top of beg ch-3—5 pineapple loops.

*Rnd 71:* Beg shell in shell, * (ch 6, sc in next ch-6 lp) 18 times; ch 6, shell in shell, ch 6, sc in first ch-3 lp, (ch 3, sc in next lp) 4 times; ch 6, shell in shell; rep from * around; join last ch-6 to top of beg ch-3—4 pineapple loops.

*Rnd 72:* Beg shell in shell, * (ch 6, sc in next ch-6 lp) 19 times; ch 6, shell in shell, ch 6, sc in first ch-3 lp, (ch 3, sc in next lp) 3 times; ch 6, shell in shell; rep from * around; join last ch-6 to top of beg ch-3—3 pineapple loops.

*Rnd 73:* Beg shell in shell, * (ch 6, sc in next ch-6 lp) 20 times; ch 6, shell in shell, ch 6, sc in first ch-3 lp, (ch 3, sc in next lp) twice; ch 6, shell in shell; rep from * around; join last ch-6 to top of beg ch-3—2 pineapple loops.

*Rnd 74:* Beg shell in shell, * (ch 6, sc in next ch-6 lp) 21 times; ch 6, shell in shell, ch 6, sc in first ch-3 lp, ch 3, sc in next lp, ch 6, shell in shell; rep from * around; join last ch-6 to top of beg ch-3—1 lp.

*Rnd 75:* Beg shell in shell, * (ch 6, sc in next ch-6 lp) 22 times; ch 6, shell in shell, dtr in ch-3 lp, 3 dc in next shell, ch 1, sl st back in ch-2 sp of previous shell, ch 1, 3 dc to finish second shell; rep from * around; ending with shell in last shell, dtr in ch-3 lp, sl st in top of ch-3 and 2 dc of first shell on rnd, sl st in ch-2 sp of shell and then sl st back into ch-2 sp of last shell made.

*Rnd 76:* Ch 9, sc in next ch-6 lp, * (ch 6, sc in next lp) 22 times; ch 6, dc in sl st where shells are joined, ch 6, sc in next ch-6 lp; rep from * around, ending with ch 3 and dc in third ch of beg ch-9.

*Rnds 77–78:* Ch 1, sc in lp just made, (ch 6, sc in next lp) all around, ending with ch 3 and dc in sc at beg of rnd. Break off at end of Rnd 78.

BLOCKING*:* On a flat surface, block with steam iron (wool setting) on wrong side, beg at center of cloth. Steam a section at a time.

# Leaves and Furrows Bedspread

Shown on page 91.
Finished size is 63x86 inches including edging.

**MATERIALS**

DMC "Brilliant" Crochet Cotton, Size 10 (50-gram balls): 30 balls ecru

Size 0 knitting needles, or size to obtain gauge given below

**Abbreviations:** Page 217.
**Gauge:** For panel B, 9 sts = 1 inch; 14 rows = 1 inch.

**INSTRUCTIONS**

**For Panel A**

Make 7. Cast on 46 sts.

*Row 1* (right side): K 1, k 2 tog, k 3, * yo, k 1, yo, k 3, sl 1, k 1, psso, k 2 tog, k 3; rep from * to last 7 sts; yo, k 1, yo, k 3, sl 1, k 1, psso, k 1.

*Row 2 and all even-numbered (wrong-side) rows:* Purl.

*Row 3:* K 1, k 2 tog, k 2, * yo, k 3, yo, k 2, sl 1, k 1, psso, k 2 tog, k 2; rep from * to last 8 sts; end yo, k 3, yo, k 2, sl 1, k 1, psso, k 1—46 sts.

*Row 5:* K 1, k 2 tog, k 1, * yo, k 5, yo, k 1, sl 1, k 1, psso, k 2 tog, k 1; rep from * to last 9 sts; end yo, k 5, yo, k 1, sl 1, k 1, psso, k 1—46 sts.

*Row 7:* K 1, k 2 tog, * yo, k 7, yo, sl 1, k 1, psso, k 2 tog; rep from * to last 10 sts; end yo, k 7, yo, sl 1, k 1, psso, k 1—46 sts.

*Row 9:* K 2, * yo, k 4, k 2 tog, k 3, yo, sl 1, k 1, psso; rep from * to last 11 sts; end yo, k 4, k 2 tog, k 3, yo, k 2—47 sts.

*Row 11:* K 2, yo, k 3, * sl 1, k 1, psso, k 2 tog, k 3, yo, k 1, yo, k 3; rep from * to last 9 sts; end sl 1, k 1, psso, k 2 tog, k 3, yo, k 2—47 sts.

*Row 13:* K 3, yo, k 2, * sl 1, k 1, psso, k 2 tog, k 2, yo, k 3, yo, k 2; rep from * to last 9 sts; end sl 1, k 1, psso, k 2 tog, k 2, yo, k 3—47 sts.

*Row 15:* K 4, yo, k 1, * sl 1, k 1, psso, k 2 tog, k 1, yo, k 5, yo, k 1; rep from * to last 9 sts; end sl 1, k 1, psso, k 2 tog, k 1, yo, k 4—47 sts.

*Row 17:* K 5, yo, * sl 1, k 1, psso, k 2 tog, yo, k 7, yo; rep from * to last 9 sts; end sl 1, k 1, psso, k 2 tog, yo, k 5—47 sts.

*Row 19:* K 1, k 2 tog, k 3, * yo, sl 1, k 1, psso, yo, k 4, k 2 tog, k 3; rep from * to last 8 sts; end yo, sl 1, k 1, psso, yo, k 4, k 2 tog—46 sts.

Rep Rows 1–20 for pat until total length measures 82 inches, ending with Row 8. Bind off.

**For panel B**

Make 8. Cast on 30 sts.

*Row 1* (right side): * K 4, p 4; rep from * across, end k 4, p 2.

*Row 2:* K 1, * p 4, k 4; rep from * across, end p 4, k 1.

*Row 3:* P 2, * k 4, p 4; rep from * across, end k 4.

*Row 4:* P 3, * k 4, p 4; rep from * across, end k 3.

*Row 5:* * P 4, k 4; rep from * across, end p 4, k 2.

*Row 6:* P 1, * k 4, p 4; rep from * across, end k 4, p 1.

*Row 7:* K 2, * p 4, k 4; rep from * across, end p 4.

*Row 8:* K 3, * p 4, k 4; rep from * across, end p 3.

Rep Rows 1–8 for pat until total length measures the same length as Panel A. Bind off.

**For the edging**

Make 4. Cast on 19 sts.

*Row 1* (wrong side): Bind off 3 sts at beg of row, (1 st rem on right-hand needle) k 1, (yo, k 2 tog) 4 times; yo, k 2, k 2 tog, yo, k 2—17 sts.

*Row 2:* K 6, p 11.

*Row 3:* K 2, (yo, k 2 tog) 4 times; yo, k 3, k 2 tog, yo, k 2—18 sts.

*Row 4:* K 6, p 12.

*continued*

*Row 5:* K 2, (yo, k 2 tog) 5 times; yo, k 2, k 2 tog, yo, k 2—19 sts.

*Row 6:* K 6, p 13. *Row 7:* P 13, k 2, k 2 tog, yo, k 2. *Row 8:* K 6, p 13.

Rep Rows 1–8 for pat until piece is length of one side of bedspread ending with Row 8. Rep edging for rem 3 sides of spread.

**To assemble**

Sew panels tog, alternating Panels A and B and positioning an A panel in center of bedspread. Sew edges to bedspread, and whipstitch ends at corners to join.

## Pineapple Popcorn Bedspread

Shown on pages 92–93.
Finished size for a twin bed is 72x108 inches plus fringe; for a double bed, 96x108 inches; and for a king-size bed, 108x108 inches.

**MATERIALS**

J & P Coats Knit-Cro-Sheen: 90 (118, 133) balls of white or ecru
Size 7 steel crochet hook

**Abbreviations:** Page 211.
**Gauge:** Each motif measures about 7 inches from side to side and 8 inches from point to point.

**INSTRUCTIONS**

*Note:* For a twin-size spread make 175 motifs, for a double-size spread make 229 motifs, for a king-size spread make 283 motifs.

**For the motif**

Starting at center, ch 8. Join with sl st to form a ring.

*Rnd 1:* Ch 3, work 17 dc in ring. Sl st in top of ch-3.

*Rnd 2:* **Ch 3, 4 dc in same place as sl st, drop lp from hook, insert hook in top of ch-3 and draw dropped lp through—starting popcorn (pc) made,** * ch 5, sk 2 dc, in next dc work **5 dc, drop lp from hook, insert hook in ch preceding the 5 dc and draw dropped lp through—popcorn made.** Rep from * around, ending ch 4, sl st in tip of beg pc.

*Rnd 3:* Work a starting pc in same place as sl st, * ch 3, dc in next sp, ch 4, pc in tip of next pc. Rep from * around, ending with ch 3, sl st in tip of first pc.

*Rnd 4:* Work a starting pc in same place as sl st, * (ch 2, dc in next ch-sp) twice; ch 3, pc in tip of next pc. Rep from * around, ending with ch 2, sl st in tip of first pc.

*Rnd 5:* Ch 3, 7 dc in same place as sl st—base of pineapple, * (ch 2, dc in next dc) twice; ch 2, 8 dc in tip of next pc. Rep from * around, ending with ch 2, sl st in top of ch-3.

*Rnd 6:* Ch 4, (dc in next dc, ch 1) 6 times; dc in next dc, * ch 2, dc in each of next 2 dc, ch 2, (dc in next dc, ch 1) 7 times; dc in next dc. Rep from * around, ending ch 2, dc in next 2 dc, ch 2, join to third ch of ch-4 at beg of rnd.

*Rnd 7:* Sl st in next ch-sp, work a starting pc in same place, (ch 2, pc in next ch-sp) 6 times; * ch 1, sk next dc, dc in next dc, ch 2, dc in next dc, ch 2, sk next dc, (pc in next ch-sp, ch 2) 6 times; pc in next ch-sp. Rep from * around, ending ch 1, sk next dc, dc in next dc, ch 2, dc in next dc, ch 1, sl st in tip of first pc.

*Rnd 8:* Sl st in next ch-sp, work a starting pc, (ch 3, pc in next sp) 5 times—6 pcs in pineapple; * (ch 2, dc in next ch-sp) 3 times, (ch 3, pc in next ch-sp) 6 times. Rep from * around—4 ch-2 sps bet pineapples; ending (ch 2, dc in next ch-sp) 3 times, ch 2, join with sl st in tip of first pc. *Rnd 9:* Work as for Rnd 8, having 5 pcs in each pineapple, and 5 ch-2 sps bet pineapples.

*Rnd 10:* * Make 4 pcs as for Rnd 8, (ch 2, dc in next ch-2 sp) 2 times, ch 2; **in next ch-2 sp work dc, ch 2, dc—inc sp made;** (ch 2, dc in next ch-2 sp) twice, ch 3. Rep from * around; ending ch 2, join to first pc.

*Rnds 11–13:* Work as for Rnd 10, making 1 less pc on each pineapple on each rnd, and working dc, ch 2 and dc in each inc sp. Join to first pc. *Rnd 14:* Sl st in next ch-sp, ch 5, * dc in next sp, ch 2. Rep from * to the inc sp, in inc sp make 3 dc, ch 2 and 3 dc; ch 2, rep from the first * around; end join with sl st to third ch of ch-5. Break off.

**To assemble the spread**

Make required number of motifs and sew together with whipstitches in the back loops of each chain.

For twin-size spread assemble 7 strips with 13 motifs and 6 strips with 14 motifs. For double-size, make 9 strips with 13 motifs and 8 strips with 14 motifs. For king-size, make 11 strips with 13 motifs and 10 strips with 14 motifs.

POPCORN MEDALLION BEDSPREAD

Twin size

For all sizes, whipstitch strips together (work in back loops), using diagram, *above*, as a guide. All sizes have short strips on both sides; strips run lengthwise on the bed.

**For the fringe**

Make fringe in each sp around as follows: Cut 8 strands, each 12 inches long. Double these strands, forming a lp. Pull lp through sp and draw loose ends through lp. Pull tight. Trim fringe evenly around.

# Tender Loving Care for Lace

Handmade lace is such a pleasure to own that it deserves the best possible care. Here are tips to help you maintain your handcrafted doilies, tablecloths, bedspreads, and other treasures so you can use and enjoy them for many years.

**Mending tears in damaged lace**

Any lace is apt to be fragile, and lace that is old, used often, or cleaned or stored incorrectly may have broken threads that need to be mended. To keep the damage from spreading, repair crocheted or knitted lace *before* washing it.

When selecting new thread to use for mending, try to match both the *color* and *weight* of the original thread. Remember that the new thread will not resemble the original thread until it has been laundered several times.

Sewing or darning may be sufficient to repair the damage. For sewing use a blunt needle, such as a tapestry needle, and insert the needle *between* the threads of the lace rather than into them.

For darning small holes, use a blunt needle. Weave horizontal threads across the tear, beginning and ending with three or more meshes on each side of the hole. Next, weave in and out of these threads, duplicating the original stitches as closely as possible.

Sometimes the damage is so severe that it can be fixed only by replacing the damaged portion. The first step before removing any of the damaged area is to place pins along each side of the lace that will be discarded and *write down the pattern used in the section you plan to remove.*

Or, find a repeat of the design within the *undamaged* portion of the lace and outline it with sewing thread so you can copy the stitches.

Next, carefully unravel the damaged portion, leaving at least two inches of thread at each end. Work these thread ends into the finished lace as you normally would on any piece of crocheting or knitting. It is important that you begin the steps on the correct side (front or back) to make the stitching match.

*For crochet,* join the new thread to the top of a stitch (chain, single crochet, or double crochet) along the right-hand edge of the damaged area. Work the stitches as established in the pattern. When you reach the opposite edge of the damaged area, join the new stitches with a slip stitch to the edge of the undamaged portion of the lace; fasten off. With a matching color of sewing thread, whipstitch the top of the repaired section to the item.

If several *rows* need to be repaired, do not fasten off. Turn the work, and crochet the next row, following your pattern. If you are working in *rounds,* join the new thread directly *above* the place previously worked; crochet across the damaged area, join the thread, and fasten off.

*For knitting,* pick up the required number of stitches from the work below the tear and reproduce the knitted portion, making sure you are on the correct side when you begin. After the knitting is finished, bind off and whipstitch the top and sides of the knitted swatch to the existing piece of lace.

**Cleaning handmade lace**

Wash crocheted or knitted lace in lukewarm water using a mild soap, and make sure the soap is completely dissolved before immersing the lace. Gently force soap suds through the lace until it is clean. Then rinse the item in cold water several times to remove the soap. Roll the lace in a towel to absorb excess moisture. (If you wash a large item, such as a bedspread, in a washing machine, be sure to use a gentle cycle.)

To shape and dry lace, pin it facedown atop a padded surface using rustproof pins. Carefully stretch and shape lace to the finished size specified in the instructions, placing pins at ½-inch intervals.

Dry the lace until slightly damp, then remove pins and carefully iron it using a press cloth and warm iron. If there are raised patterns such as bobbles or popcorns in the lace, press with the raised work facedown over heavy toweling.

*Starch lace* using liquid or spray starches. For a stiff finish, cooked starch works best; follow manufacturer's instructions. Spray starches will add crispness to lace without making it stiff. Rinse lace in liquid starch *before* blocking and drying. Use spray starches *after* lace is blocked and dried.

*Remove stains* using a gentle bleach, such as lemon juice mixed with water, or hydrogen peroxide diluted according to the manufacturer's directions. Or, use a weak solution of nonchlorine household bleach. Begin with one teaspooon of bleach per cup of water. Soak lace only long enough to remove the stain.

Home dry cleaning will remove some stains that won't disappear in water solutions. Before applying a dry-cleaning product, read the label directions carefully.

**Storing handmade lace**

Store your knitted or crocheted laces in a cool, dry place. Lay small pieces flat, without folding, between sheets of acid-free tissue paper or cotton muslin. Loosely roll larger pieces around a cardboard or wooden cylinder that has been wrapped with tissue paper or muslin. Wrap another layer of tissue paper around the outside of the lace. Avoid storing lace in plastic bags.

# BORROWING DESIGNS FROM OTHER CRAFTS

***Patterns and motifs derived from other needlecrafts—such as patchwork and embroidery—suggest exciting new design possibilities for crocheters and knitters.***

The strong graphics and subtle colorations of a traditional Amish quilt design (the Diamond-in-Square, *below*) inspired the boldly patterned afghan shown at *right.* Intriguing stitch variations are introduced with each new color change in this 42-inch-square crocheted design, evoking the richly textured surface typical of exceptional Amish quilting.

Stitch instructions are on page 203.